The Lord in Us

The Lord in Us

IF YOU CAN LOVE AN ENEMY, YOU CAN LOVE ANYONE

Chad Tucker

NEW HARBOR PRESS

COLORADO SPRINGS, CO

Tucker/New Harbor Press
13395 Voyager Pkwy, Ste 130
Colorado Springs, CO 80921
www.newharborpress.com

Ordering Information:
Quantity sales. Special discounts are available on quantity pur-
chases by corporations, associations, and others. For details,
contact the "Special Sales Department" at the address above.

The Lord in Us/ Chad Tucker. -- 1st ed.
ISBN 978-1-63357-160-0

Contents

And so we know and rely on the love God has for us. God is love. Whoever lives in love lives in God, and God in them.

1 John 4:16 NIV

Love is patient, love is kind. It does not envy, it does not boast, it is not proud. It does not dishonor others, it is not self-seeking, it is not easily angered, it keeps no record of wrongs. Love does not delight in evil but rejoices with the truth. It always protects, always trusts, always hopes, always perseveres. Love never fails.

1 Corinthians 13:4-8 NIV

For those God foreknew He also predestined to be conformed to the image of His Son, that He might be the firstborn among many brothers and sisters.

Romans 8:29 NIV

Acknowledgments

I would like to thank first and foremost God, Jesus Christ, and the Holy Spirit for everything I have been blessed with. I want to give a special thanks to my mother who has always been my greatest fan, and had it not been for her, the seed of faith in God may have never been planted in me during the years of my youth. I would like to thank my first pastor, Ray Bentley, from Maranatha Chapel in San Diego. He was always a great inspiration to me from the time I was eighteen years old, and I wish I had gone to church more often during my young adult years.

I also would like to thank my dad for doing his best to keep me out of trouble. I can now thank him for his strict discipline, and I know he was a better dad to me than my grandfather was to him. He was a good provider until I was eighteen and helped me very much with my education. I would like to thank my oldest brother who has always been very protective and my other brother for his help in changing my life when I was seventeen years old.

I would like to thank all of my friends from the past and now in the present; especially those who stayed friends with me even when I was at my worst. I would like to thank the Bibbs, Whittingtons, Nothwangs, and the Rineharts for welcoming me into their homes and treating me like family – I miss you all very much.

Last but not least, I am very grateful for Pastor Larry Johnson from The Training Center, Pastor Daryl Kyle Sr. from Calvary Chapel Perfect Love, Pastor William Marrs Jr., John Williams – my sobriety mentor, Kimberly – my dear friend and sister in the Lord, and all the fellow believers that are in my family circle now. You all know who you are and I wouldn't be where I am today without all of your support.

Introduction

I want to start out by thanking anyone who may have an interest in this book. In my opinion, it is a book for anyone interested in the Lord and in the teachings of Jesus Christ. In this chaotic world there are many distractions from what I consider to be most important in life and that is God the Father, Jesus Christ, and the Holy Spirit. Without these three in your life it is basically like living, as you may have heard, on sinking sand. If you are new to hearing about the gospel of Jesus Christ, I recommend you start reading the book of Matthew in the New Testament of the Holy Bible. If you have a little faith, you are well on your way to an eternal life.

I chose the title of this book to remind those who believe in Jesus Christ that, if we live in love, we live in God and God lives in us. I also chose this title because it has been my most personal favorite verse now for a long time (1 John 4:16).

When I first read this verse, it amazed me. At one point in my life, I questioned myself, "If you could pick one word that would best describe the Holy Bible, what word would you choose?" Some people could say Jesus, God, miracles, or heaven, but I always thought of the word, love. So, when I read this verse, I decided that this will be my life-long favorite verse.

I still can't memorize the complete verse off the top of my head, but I always remember the main part of it: God is love. Whoever lives in love lives in God and God in them. What an amazing truth! But how do we abide in love? Well first of all, love is defined in 1 Corinthians 13:4-8 as noted at the beginning of this book, and we can learn more about how to love by the words of Jesus Christ in the gospels of Matthew, Mark, Luke, and John in the Holy Bible. If we are to learn anything about love, Jesus Christ is the perfect example.

I believe love is powerful. I believe it is also feared. I remember seeing an old friend from high school when I was in my twenties, and we were out in front of a bar, and he was so happy to see me that he wanted to give me a hug, but my pride wasn't having it. I actually remember pushing him away. At that time in my life I was not one to give hugs to another man. I was very much filled with pride. I believe pride fights off any love offered. Giving love and receiving love requires vulnerability. It's like going against the grain of human nature

I was brought up to be rough and tough as a way of protecting myself. The world teaches self-defense while Jesus says to turn the other cheek. The world says to be proud while Jesus says to be humble. The only way we are ever going to even come close to walking the talk of love is by the power of the Holy Spirit in our lives.

If you are a believer and you feel like you are struggling in your walk to follow Jesus, remember Romans 9:20, "But who are you, a human being, to talk back to God? Shall what is formed say to the one who formed it, Why did you make me like this? Does not the potter have the right to make out of the same lump of clay some pottery for special purposes and some for common use?"

We all fall short of the glory of God. In our weaknesses, God is strong. His power is made perfect in weakness (2 Corinthians 12:9). Our shortcomings help us to stay humble. I encourage you to pray often after the manner Jesus spoke of:

And when you pray, do not be like the hypocrites, for they love to pray standing in the synagogues and on the street corners to be seen by others. Truly I tell you, they have their reward in full. But when you pray, go into your room, close the door and pray to your Father, who is unseen. Then your Father, who sees what is done in secret, will reward you. And when you pray, do not keep on babbling like pagans, for they think they will be heard because of their many words. Do not be like them, for your Father knows what you need before you ask Him. This, then, is how you should pray: "Our Father in heaven, hallowed by your name, your kingdom come, your will be done, on earth as it is in heaven. Give us today our daily bread. And forgive us our debts, as we also have forgiven our debtors. And lead us not into temptation, but deliver us from the evil one." (Matthew 6:5-13)

Pray at all times , and remember that Christ is at the right hand of God and is interceding for us

(Romans 8:34). The Bible says that the Holy Spirit will teach us all things (John 14:26), maybe even some of those mysteries of the kingdom Jesus spoke of. Study to show yourself approved unto God (2 Timothy 2:15). We believers are being conformed to the image and likeness of Jesus (Romans 8:29) Pray for patience. God's timing is eternal, not just a lifetime.

The children of God press on toward the goal to win the prize for which God has called us heavenward in Christ Jesus (Philippians 3:14). Where your treasure is there your heart will be also (Matthew 6:21). I think we should focus more on where our heart is rather than where our treasure is. If you want to abide in love, I suggest this: focus on your enemies first. <u>If you can love an enemy, you can love anyone</u>. The devil is our greatest enemy, and he is the only exception to the rule of loving our enemies. We cannot serve two masters, either we will hate the one and love the other, or be devoted to the one and despise the other (Matthew 6:24). He's the craftiest beast ever created. I believe we will find out why he was even created to begin with when we get to heaven. The Lord declared, "My thoughts are not your thoughts, neither are your ways my ways" (Isaiah 55:8).

In this book, I will provide verses from the Holy Bible that touch on some very important topics regarding our walk in faith and belief in Jesus Christ. Jesus said, "Whoever wants to be my disciple must deny themselves and take up their cross and follow me" (Luke 9:23). We need the word of God and the help of the Holy Spirit to follow Him. He told the fishermen 2000 years ago that they will fish for men and that is my intention of writing this book – I'm casting this biblical information out into the world hoping that the gospel of Christ can reach the hearts of many men and women.

I will share my testimony because I believe that it will shine a light of hope to others and let them know that the bible and Jesus can take us out of our darkest valleys in life and bring us into the light where we can find peace and rest. There is victory over the devil in sharing our testimonies as you will see from a bible verse written at the beginning of the next chapter. If you are interested in salvation from God's wrath that is to come, please pray this short and simple prayer with me:

Dear Heavenly Father,

I am terribly sorry for all the wrong things I have done in my life and I confess that I am a sinner. I now profess with my mouth that Jesus Christ is Lord and believe in my heart that You raised Him from the dead. Thank you for my salvation and help me to follow Jesus all the days of my life.

If you have said this prayer, Romans 10:9 declares that you now have salvation through Jesus Christ. I recommend you find a local church that studies the word of God thoroughly and be baptized as soon as possible. Welcome into the family of God!

Ephesians 6:12 states, "for our struggle is not against flesh and blood, but against the rulers, against the authorities, against the powers of this dark world and against the spiritual forces of evil in the heavenly realms." I pray that God the Father, Jesus Christ, and the Holy Spirit will put a hedge of protection around you, your family, and friends. I pray that God will give His angels charge concerning you and them. I also pray that this book encourages and edifies those who read it and that God, Jesus Christ, and the Holy Spirit might be glorified by it.

CHAPTER ONE

My Testimony

They triumphed over him [the devil] by the blood of the Lamb and by the word of their testimony; they did not love their lives so much as to shrink from death.
Revelation 12:11

When I was fifteen years old I had my first experience with "the cross." I was at my friend's house, and he was attempting to tattoo himself with just a regular needle and ink. I decided to join in and quickly tattooed a small cross on my left knuckle. I didn't attend church regularly at that time. My mother had taken me to church once, and I knew she believed in God so I just followed suit.

My mother has always been a very loving and nurturing person, and I could always see the light in her. My brothers and I didn't have to go to church because my father was (and still is) an atheist. He told my mother we would only be brainwashed if she took us to church but today I realize that a good "brainwash" was probably what we needed the most. There's nothing wrong with renewing the minds of young children and teenagers, right?

When I turned seventeen, my middle brother introduced me to the movie *Jesus of Nazareth*, and I bawled. This movie had a very strong impact on my life, and to be honest, I consider it to be the greatest movie of all time. My brother was "on fire" as they would say for a young twenty year old but was still fighting some of his own demons. But one thing was for sure, he believed in Jesus Christ and the Holy Bible. He asked me if I wanted to be baptized and I agreed. My parents had one of those large jacuzzi-style tubs, and I was ready. I'll never forget that day. I got in the tub and my brother said, "I now baptize you in the name of the Father, the Son, and the Holy Ghost" and under I went. I didn't even know the significance or symbolism of that action until many years later. All I know is when I came up out of the water my brother asked me, "What do you see?" I quickly replied, "I see pain."

I didn't know this scripture at the time I got baptized but it says, "The Spirit Himself testifies with our spirit that we are God's children. Now if we are children, then we are heirs – heirs of God and co-heirs with Christ, <u>if indeed we share in His sufferings</u> in order that we may also share in His glory. I consider that our present sufferings are not worth comparing with the glory that will be revealed in us" (Romans 8:16-18).

I had no idea at that moment just how much suffering I was going to have to endure. I had a full-time job, and when I didn't have to work, I would just surf and work out at the gym. I was just a young, ignorant man who thought he knew it all. If I had only known the pain I was going to experience in the future because of self-will, lust, addiction, pride, selfishness, and the love of money. I was a young believer but had authority issues, no fear of the Lord, and no sense of obedience.

When I turned eighteen, my parents told me they were going to get a divorce, so I was in a hurry to get my own place with a young woman, married or unmarried. I had asked my first true love from sixth grade if she would marry me, and she agreed. But shortly after she said yes, I couldn't get ahold of her for some reason. She basically just disappeared. I started fornicating with different women and started to feel conviction. I thought to myself, I need to get married. I wanted to marry the first girl I asked, but she flew the coop. So I then ended up starting a relationship (on the rebound) with a friend from work. We started going to church together, and we quickly got married when we were eighteen years old.

When I asked her to marry me, it was basically so I wouldn't fornicate anymore, and I knew she would be a loving partner to me. But I failed to think about just how much I really loved her. During our marriage my eyes would wander. On more than one occasion, I would break up and say I wanted out and then go back to her out of pity. It was doomed from the start. I felt stuck, I felt guilty if I stayed with her and guilty if I left her. I finally ended the relationship because she wanted to start taking fertility injections and having children. I was only making $8/hour and was not in a position to start a family. Her path was going one way and my path was going another. She may not have got married for the wrong reasons, but I definitely did.

We finally divorced when I was twenty-three years old. I remember telling her that I just didn't think I loved her the way a husband should love his wife. I knew the first girl I asked to marry was the one I really wanted to be with but she was nowhere to be found at the time.

After the divorce, the devil took me for a ride. I thought I was finally free. I didn't have to go to church on Sundays anymore; I could go surfing or fishing instead. I remember being so elated singing to the band, Rush, "I will choose free will!" I even stopped believing in Jesus after taking an Anthropology course at a community college and learning about the theory of evolution. I had a plan. I was going to go out to bars and clubs, and I was going to find the perfect mate.

So, all the fornication started over, and by the time I was twenty-five, I found "the one." It lasted six months and was a crazy relationship, so crazy that we ended up in the office of a psychologist to counsel us. The counseling did not work. He turned me on to many psychology books but now I know none of them hold a candle to the Holy Bible. I even read a book I found on my own called *Romancing the Shadow—Illuminating the Dark Side of the Soul*. Not a book I would recommend today. I was on the wrong path going further and further away from Jesus. I started slipping into fits of anger, psychosis, and depression. Shortly after the breakup I went on a downward spiral, became homeless, and was diagnosed with Schizoaffective Disorder which was definitely a hard pill to swallow. Schizoaffective Disorder is a mental illness that displays symptoms of both Schizophrenia and Bipolar Disorder. My pride did not want to accept the fact that I had a mental illness.

But something good did happen after that last breakup. I started having interest in Jesus again. I remember reading the book, *The Road Less Traveled*, and it kind of reignited my faith. I started to receive Social Security Disability Income, and it helped me get off the streets at the age of twenty-six. I stayed in a very slum hotel in downtown San Diego. I had some money, but I didn't have a vehicle. I was very depressed because I had lost everything and was feeling very hopeless and alone. I was so depressed that I took a bunch of pills in that small hotel room and just wanted to die. I thought I could just go home to heaven on my own terms but it didn't work. I tried it two more times, once at the age of thirty-one and the last time at the age of thirty-four. I was going to try one more time at the age of forty-three but I heard a voice speak to my heart, urging me not to try it ever again. I believe it was the Holy Spirit. The voice warned of a possible consequence if I tried. I later learned that the Lord disciplines those He loves.

I grew marijuana on several occasions. Marijuana was an idol to me. Women, marijuana, and surfing were all idols that I worshipped unawares. I went through periods where it would look like I was doing better and then I would have a breakdown and lose everything. I couldn't tell you how many times I had to start all over and get back on my feet. I was homeless many times. I've been homeless in San Diego mostly, also in Los Angeles and Florida. I ended up in and out of jail over the years for petty theft (homeless), wet and reckless, trespassing, vehicle theft (homeless), and the last time I was found not guilty and the charges were dismissed for public intoxication and resisting arrest (I was just homeless again and in bad shape). I also was taken to psychiatric hospitals by the police on more than one occasion (5150's). I basically visited just about every psychiatric hospital in San Diego. I also remember visits to two psychiatric hospitals in Las Vegas, Nevada.

I actually thought I didn't have a drug problem. I started drinking alcohol and smoking marijuana at the age of eleven. I began experimenting with crystal, mushrooms, and LSD at the age of fifteen. In my adult years I dabbled with cocaine and smoked heroin a couple times but didn't enjoy the heroin. At the time, I thought I was having "good times," the partying, the drugs, the surfing, the fishing, the women; but what was I sowing in all of that? <u>We reap what we sow</u>. Teach that concept to a young man or woman and watch what happens. Even though sometimes I was happy, it was not the joy of the Lord I experience today.

God has definitely carried me through the hard times, especially homelessness. I was lost in Los Angeles with clouds in the sky, and I couldn't even tell where the sun was to determine which way was west. I knew I needed to go west and then south, back to San Diego. The bus drivers let me on sometimes when I didn't have money. Sometimes, I had to sleep somewhere during the day and walk at night to avoid the cold. One night I remember sleeping on cardboard in a dumpster in Florida. I was walking the streets of East Los Angeles in the middle of the night in places you would never imagine. At night there were no restrooms available, and one time I defecated in a park. At one point I threw away my socks because they were so dirty. Then shortly after, I threw away my boots because they were just rubbing my feet raw. I've walked many miles homeless on the streets but luckily I rarely had to walk in the rain. I never got rest at night, never. I suffered sleep deprivation many times when I was homeless and it would put me into a state of psychosis. But there were angels that helped me out along the way. I know they were angels. Remember; "do not forget to show hospitality to strangers, for by so doing some people have shown hospitality to angels without knowing it" (Hebrews 13:2)

During my last visit in jail, something miraculous happened. I remember praying and telling God that, if I had known that being a Christian was going to be this hard, I would have never started the process of belief. I was suffering so bad that I told the Father, "Until you help me, I am going to be angry at Jesus!" That was the first time I had ever felt angry with my Savior. I felt utterly hopeless, and all the suffering I was going through was starting to make me question my faith. But the Father heard that prayer of mine, and I received help from others that I so desperately needed. I used the Son against the Father, and the Father made sure that my anger with my Savior would not last long.

Something happened to me in jail shortly after that prayer. I had been planning on smoking marijuana when I got out of jail, especially because it had just been legalized recreationally in California. A faith-based visitor insisted that it would be in my best interest to give up the marijuana, and I basically told him it would take a miracle for me to quit smoking pot. I remember when he was speaking to me during the visit, I began to cry, and I can't even remember what sparked it. Maybe it was because he was a sincere marriage and family therapist who was trying to help. Maybe I was crying because I was contemplating changing my life. I'm not sure to this day. All I know is that I was tired of the train wreck I had been on and I was completely broken. My past twenty years had been littered with hardships, confusion, mental illness, and depression, and I didn't know what to do.

As I returned to my jail cell and the door closed, the miracle happened. I felt a rush of anger, and I threw my cup against the wall. Then, I quickly realized the therapist was right. It was like a light came on in my head, and I started thinking rationally. I immediately made a decision that I was going to quit smoking marijuana and drinking beer, and that I was going to get clean and stay sober for one reason—1 Peter 5:8 which says, "Be alert and of sober mind. Your enemy the devil prowls around like a roaring lion looking for someone to devour." I had been reading the bible while I was in jail and that verse was planted in my mind along with two other verses: The Lord is close to the brokenhearted and saves those who are crushed in spirit (Psalm 34:18) and the Lord disciplines the one He loves (Hebrews 12:6).

I looked at all my times of homelessness, jail, and psychiatric hospital visits as times that He was disciplining me, and I didn't want to be disciplined anymore. I finally realized that I was holding on to beer and marijuana so tight and I needed to let them go. Later I learned that they were idols that I was worshipping for far too long. Today I'm 46 years old and by the grace of God I've been completely sober for two years. That's a long time to be sober for someone with a history of addiction. Hopefully, by the grace of God I can continue on in my sobriety.

There were many times that I would mourn from the age of seventeen to forty-three. I held onto the verse that says, "those who sow with tears will reap with songs of joy" (Psalm 126:5). I always remembered the verses, "blessed are those who mourn, for they will be comforted" (Matthew 5:4), and "our present sufferings are not worth comparing with the glory that will be revealed in us" (Romans 8:18). I would often ask God how long must I suffer? The bible says that Jesus came "that they may have life, and have it to the full" (John 10:10). I never understood what that meant because I was going through so much depression. I understand now the life I wanted in the past was not the life God wanted for me.

During my last time in jail I made a decision that I was going to start honoring my father and mother. It had been hard to listen to what my dad would suggest because he was an atheist and I was a believer. They both wanted me to be sober, and my dad had already told me not to even contact him until I had a year of sobriety. This comes from an atheist who drinks Jack Daniels and Coke occasionally. That was hard for me but I did it anyway. I ended up calling him on his birthday to tell him I had been sober a year. He asked me how I did it, and I told him, "I know you don't want me to talk about the bible or religion but I did it with the help of God." My mother is overjoyed by the difference in me and says, "I got my son back." I told her that all her prayers regarding me were finally answered. She tells me she's proud of me today, and I just give the glory to Christ. She had been fighting against my addiction to marijuana for nearly thirty years.

In addition to getting completely sober, I also had to come to terms with my mental illness. For the past twenty years, I never took my diagnosis seriously. I would take my medication at first but then I would stop, thinking I really didn't need it. I have found out through trial and error that I definitely need to take the medication prescribed to me by my doctor on a consistent basis and it clearly says not to take this medication with alcohol. There were too many times that I would stop taking my medication, and I would then become unstable and many times, homeless. After my first year of being sober, I thought I didn't need my medication, and I ended up leaving where I lived and just started walking the streets with a suitcase and a backpack. Now I take my medication as prescribed, and I live a very stable life. I just finally came to a point of acceptance to the fact that my mind is not wired healthy and normal like others. God uses medicine and doctors to help people. It's like someone who has a heart condition and takes medicine. The only difference is that my problem is located in the brain.

Today I can honestly say that I really don't suffer. The joy of the Lord is my strength (Nehemiah 8:10), and He gives me rest now. Jesus Christ's yoke is easy and His burden is light (Matthew 11:30). I'm constantly praying God's will be done even if it's going to be difficult. But that's the thing, it hasn't been difficult. I've never had so much rest or peace in my life. As I start to attempt to write this book, I'm praying the Lord speaks to me and guides me by the Holy Spirit. If it is God's will for me to complete the task of writing a book, let it be done for His glory. I see life with different eyes now. God has given me a certain measure of discernment. I believe I was born again January 23, 2017 which involves the mysteries of the kingdom of God. I believe God put the Holy Spirit in me when I tattooed that cross on my knuckle. There have been times where I felt the fear of the Lord, and I believe that was the baptism of fire.

I now live in Spring Valley, California which is about twenty minutes from downtown San Diego. I no longer have idols in my life and have been delivered from fornication. I'm in fellowship with many other believers (mostly men) and can attend a fellowship meeting practically any day of the week. I used to believe you can only count your true friends on one hand but I don't believe that anymore. I've been adopted into a huge family and there are many people I can go to for support. I work for one of my pastors as an assistant manager of a faith-based apartment complex. We are currently in the process of turning this complex into a large family of believers who maintain sobriety. I've been blessed beyond measure. I am truly surrounded by the love of Christ in this community. I'm excited to see what more the Lord has planned for those who love Him and who are called according to His purpose (Romans 8:28). I pray that you might take something from my testimony and somehow be edified by this book. May you be blessed overwhelmingly by God the Father, Jesus Christ, and the Holy Spirit.

CHAPTER TWO

The Father, the Son, and the Holy Spirit

Jesus referred to the Holy Spirit as the Helper. He said that it is to our advantage that He goes away so that the Holy Spirit will come to us. The Helper or Holy Spirit was sent by the Father after His resurrection, and Jesus said that the Holy Spirit will teach us all things (John14:26). The Holy Spirit is a person, not just a force or thing. There is unity between God the Father, the Son, and the Holy Spirit.

I believe we can access the mysteries of the kingdom of heaven by the power and indwelling of the Holy Spirit. Jesus said that the kingdom of heaven is in your midst (Luke 17:21). By the power of the Holy Spirit we can tap into the supernatural, unconditional love of God. God loves us more than we can comprehend. He is merciful, gracious, and slow to anger. He is patient with us and rejoices with the angels when a sinful man or woman repents.

He gives us free will, and if we don't make the right choices in life, He will discipline us and try to get our attention:

"Do not despise the Lord's discipline, and do not resent His rebuke, because the Lord disciplines those He loves, as a father the son he delights in. Blessed are those who find wisdom, those who gain understanding, for she is more profitable than silver and yields better returns than gold.... Her ways are pleasant ways, and all her paths are peace" (Proverbs 3:11-17). We have to give respect, honor, and reverence to our heavenly Father who corrects us.

There have been many times I have knelt in reverence to God and prayed. But when you look how Jesus prayed in the Garden of Gethsemane, He fell on His face before God and prayed. Have you ever prayed in that position? The Son of Man, one with the Father, became a little lower than the angels. The King of Kings and Lord of Lords humbled Himself and came to serve rather than be served. He washed the disciples' feet, and He was baptized by John the Baptist when John felt he should be baptized by Him.

God is love. Jesus is love. The Holy Spirit is love. The three are one. For those of us who believe in Jesus, all three are in us. What power of love we have access to! Love is the challenge of Jesus. Jesus had two commandments: Love the Father and love your neighbor as yourself (Matthew 22:37-39). For the entire law is fulfilled in keeping this one command: Love your neighbor as yourself (Galatians 5:14).

We overcome by the blood of the lamb and by the word of our testimonies. We overcome by Jesus's victory over sin that took place 2,000 years ago. We are the light of the world, and we need the love of Christ to be perfected in us. "Perfect love drives out fear" (1 John 4:18). We need to pray for the ability not to just talk about love but to live it out in our everyday lives. Daily, we are tested and challenged to love our neighbors and enemies. I know for me personally, some days I fail miserably, and some days I don't. It's a matter of the heart. Jesus said, "Do not harden your hearts." We are to have bowels of mercy. In 1 John 4:20 it says, "Whoever claims to love God yet hates a brother or sister is a liar. For whoever does not love their brother and sister, whom they have seen, cannot love God, whom they have not seen."

I've only been a new creation for a year and a half since I was born again, and I know my heart is changing more and more every day. I lived about forty-four years before I was born again so it is going to take some time and patience for my transformation and the renewing of my mind. I still struggle with the temptations of lust and my flesh wars against the spirit every day. But I'm already seeing a change; the spirit is winning and the flesh is losing.

I believe we have more power than we think. It's not our power though. We have the Father, the Son, and the Holy Spirit on our side at all times. Daily, we are in a war with the devil, his angels, and demons. The objective of the devil is to steal, kill, and destroy. (John 10:10) He's the father of lies and the deceiver. The demise of the devil is found in Revelation 20:10, "And the devil, who deceived them, was thrown into the lake of burning sulfur, where the beast and the false prophet had been thrown. They will be tormented day and night for ever and ever." If you ever hear the enemy in your head, condemning you, trying to make you feel guilt or shame, just remind him of Revelation 20:10. "Resist the devil, and he will flee from you" (James 4:7). I believe our greatest mistakes or regrets that we have made in our lives were probably because we were deceived by the devil just as Eve was in the garden of Eden.

~God, the Father~

In the beginning God created the heavens and the earth. (Genesis 1:1)

God is faithful; he will not let you be tempted beyond what you can bear. But when you are tempted, He will also provide a way out so that you can endure it. (1 Corinthians 10:13)

God is light; in Him there is no darkness at all. (1 John 1:5)

The Lord is not slow in keeping His promise, as some understand slowness. Instead He is patient with us, not wanting anyone to perish, but everyone to come to repentance. (2 Peter 3:9)

For the word of God is alive and active. Sharper than any double-edged sword, it penetrates even to dividing soul and spirit, joints and marrow; it judges the thoughts and attitudes of the heart. (Hebrews 4:12)

Every good and perfect gift is from above, coming down from God and the heavenly lights, which does not change like shifting shadows. (James 1:17)

For God so loved the world that He gave His one and only Son, that whoever believes in him shall not perish but have eternal life. (John 3:16)

God is spirit, and His worshipers must worship in the Spirit and in truth. (John 4:24)

Look at the birds of the air; they do not sow or reap or store away in barns, and yet your Heavenly Father feeds them. Are you not much more valuable than they? (Matthew 6:26)

God is not human that He should lie, not a human being, that he should change His mind. Does He speak and then not act? Does He promise and not fulfill? (Numbers 23:19)

As for God, His way is perfect: the Lord's word is flawless; He shields all who take refuge in Him. (Psalm 18:30)

And the heavens proclaim His righteousness, for He is a God of justice. (Psalm 50:6)

God is gracious and righteous; our God is full of compassion. (Psalm 116:5)

For the wages of sin is death, but the gift of God is eternal life in Christ Jesus our Lord. (Romans 6:23)

Praise be to the Lord, to God our Savior, who daily bears our burdens. Our God is a God who saves; from the Sovereign Lord comes escape from death. (Psalm 68:19-20)

For the Lord God is a sun and shield: the Lord bestows favor and honor; no good thing does He withhold from those whose walk is blameless. Lord Almighty, blessed is the one who trusts in you. (Psalm 84:11-12)

Who is a God like you, who pardons sin and forgives the transgression of the remnant of his inheritance? You do not stay angry forever but delight to show mercy. You will again have compassion on us; you will tread our sins underfoot and hurl all our iniquities into the depths of the sea. (Micah 7:18-19)

Hear, O Israel: The Lord our God, the Lord is one. Love the Lord your God with all your heart and with all your soul and with all your strength. (Deuteronomy 6:4-5)

Dear friends, let us love one another, for love comes from God. Everyone who loves has been born of God and knows God. Whoever does not love does not know God, because God is love. This is how God showed His love among us:

He sent His one and only Son into the world that we might live through Him. (1 John 4:7-9)

In the last days I will pour out my Spirit on all people. Your sons and daughters will prophesy, your young men will see visions, your old men will dream dreams. (Acts 2:17)

~Quotes of Jesus, the Son of God~

For whoever does the will of my Father in heaven is my brother and sister and mother. (Matthew 12:50)

Whoever wants to be first must be slave of all. For even the Son of Man did not come to be served, but to serve, and to give His life as a ransom for many. (Mark 10:44-45)

For those who exalt themselves will be humbled, and those who humble themselves will be exalted. (Matthew 23:12)

Come, follow me, and I will send you out to fish for people. (Matthew 4:19)

Therefore I tell you, whatever you ask for in prayer, believe that you have received it, and it will be yours. And when you stand praying, if you hold anything against anyone, forgive them, so that your Father in heaven may forgive you your sins. (Mark 11:24-25)

So do not worry, saying, "What shall we eat?" or "What shall we drink?" or "What shall we wear?" For the pagans run after all these things, and your heavenly Father knows that you need them. But seek first His kingdom and His righteousness, and all these things will be given to you as well. Therefore do not worry about tomorrow, for tomorrow will worry about itself. Each day has enough trouble of its own. (Matthew 6:31-34)

Blessed are those who are persecuted because of righteousness, for theirs is the kingdom of heaven. (Matthew 5:10)

What do you think? If a man owns a hundred sheep, and one of them wanders away, will he not leave the ninety-nine on the hills and go to look for the one that wandered off? And if he finds it, truly I tell you, he is happier about that one sheep than about the ninety-nine that did not wander off. In the same way your Father in heaven is not willing that any of these little ones should perish. (Matthew 18:12-14)

Blessed are you when people insult you, persecute you and falsely say all kinds of evil against you because of me. Rejoice and be glad, because great is your reward in heaven, for in the same way they persecuted the prophets who were before you. (Matthew 5:11-12)

Whoever drinks of the water I give to them will never thirst. Indeed, the water I give them will become in them a spring of water welling up to eternal life. (John 4:14)

The thief comes only to steal and kill and destroy; I have come that they may have life, and have it to the full. I am the good shepherd. The good shepherd lays down His life for the sheep. (John 10:10-11)

I am the way and the truth and the life. No one comes to the Father except through me. (John 14:6)

Let the little children come to me, and do not hinder them, for the kingdom of heaven belongs to such as these. (Matthew 19:14)

It is not the healthy who need a doctor, but the sick. I have not come to call the righteous, but sinners to repentance. (Luke 5:31-32)

Whoever wants to be my disciple must deny themselves and take up their cross and follow me. For whoever wants to save their life will lose it, but whoever loses their life for me and for the gospel will save it. What good is it for someone to gain the whole world, yet forfeit their soul? Or what can anyone give in exchange for their soul? (Mark 8:34-37)

Let your light shine before others, that they may see your good deeds and glorify your Father in heaven. (Matthew 5:16)

You have heard that it was said, "Love your neighbor and hate your enemy." But I tell you, love your enemies and pray for those who persecute you. (Matthew 5:43-44)

So in everything, do to others what you would have them do to you, for this sums up the Law and the Prophets. (Matthew 7:12)

Love the Lord your God with all your heart and with all your soul and with all your mind. This is the first and greatest commandment. And the second is like it: Love your neighbor as yourself. All the Law and the Prophets hang on these two commandments. (Matthew 22:37-40)

I have told you these things, so that in me you may have peace. In this world you will have trouble. But take heart! I have overcome the world. (John 16:33)

The harvest is plentiful but the workers are few. (Matthew 9:37)

Take my yoke upon you and learn from me, for I am gentle and humble in heart and you will find rest for your souls. For my yoke is easy and my burden is light. (Matthew 11:29-30)

With God all things are possible. (Matthew 19:26)

The Holy Spirit...will teach you all things. (John 14:26)

I and the Father are one. (John 10:30)

~The Holy Spirit~

Through Christ Jesus the law of the Spirit who gives life has set you free from the law of sin and death. For what the law was powerless to do because it was weakened by the flesh, God did by sending His own Son in the likeness of sinful flesh to be a sin offering. And so he condemned sin in the flesh, in order that the righteous requirement of the law might be fully met in us, who do not live according to the flesh but according to the Spirit. Those who live according to the flesh have their minds set on what the flesh desires; but those who live in accordance with the Spirit have their minds set on what the Spirit desires. The mind governed by the flesh is death, but the mind governed by the Spirit is life and peace. (Romans 8:2-6)

They went out from us, but they did not really belong to us. For if they had belonged to us, they would have remained with us; but their going showed that none of them belonged to us. But you have an anointing from the Holy One, and all of you know the truth. I do not write to you because you do not know the truth, but because you do know it and because no lie comes from the truth. (1 John 2:19-21)

Who is the liar? It is whoever denies that Jesus is the Christ. Such a person is the antichrist—denying the Father and the Son. No one who denies the Son has the Father; whoever acknowledges the Son has the Father also. As for you, see that what you have heard from the beginning remains in you. If it does, you also will remain in the Son and in the Father. And this is what He promised us—eternal life. I am writing these things to you about those who are trying to lead you astray. As for you, the anointing you received from Him remains in you, and you do not need anyone to teach you. But as His anointing teaches you about all things and as that anointing is real, not counterfeit—just as it has taught you, remain in Him. (1 John 2:22-27)

Do you not know that your bodies are temples of the Holy Spirit, who is in you, whom you have received from God? You are not your own; you were bought at a price. Therefore honor God with your bodies. (1 Corinthians 6:19-20)

Now the Lord is the Spirit, and where the Spirit of the Lord is, there is freedom. (2 Corinthians 3:17)

CHAPTER THREE

The Fruit of the Spirit

You, my brothers and sisters, were called to be free. But do not use your freedom to indulge the flesh; rather, serve one another humbly in love. For the entire law is fulfilled in keeping this one command: "Love your neighbor as yourself." If you bite and devour each other, watch out or you will be destroyed by each other. (Galatians 5:13-15)

So I say, walk by the Spirit, and you will not gratify the desires of the flesh. For the flesh desires what is contrary to the Spirit, and the Spirit what is contrary to the flesh. They are in conflict with each other, so that you are not to do whatever you want. But if you are led by the Spirit, you are not under the law. (Galatians 5:16-18)

The acts of the flesh are obvious: sexual immorality, impurity and debauchery; idolatry and witchcraft; hatred, discord, jealousy, fits of rage, selfish ambition, dissensions, factions and envy; drunkenness, orgies, and the like. I warn you, as I did before, that those who live like this will not inherit the kingdom of God. (Galatians 5:19-21)

But the fruit of the Spirit is love, joy, peace, forbearance, kindness, goodness, faithfulness, gentleness and self-control. Against such things there is no law. Those who belong to Christ Jesus have crucified the flesh with its passions and desires. Since we live by the Spirit, let us keep in step with the Spirit. Let us not become conceited, provoking and envying each other. (Galatians 5:22-26)

~Love~

Love is patient, love is kind. It does not envy, it does not boast, it is not proud. It does not dishonor others, it is not self-seeking, it is not easily angered, it keeps no record of wrongs. Love does not delight in evil but rejoices with the truth. It always protects, always trusts, always hopes, always perseveres. Love never fails. (1 Corinthians 13:4-8)

~Joy~

Joy is a delight of the mind or passion and emotion excited by a rational prospect of possessing what we love or desire. To be joyful is to be glad or rejoice.

~Peace~

Peace is a state of quiet or tranquil freedom from disturbance or agitation of the mind.

~Forbearance~

Forbearance is the exercise of patience or long suffering. Patience is a calm temper which bears evils or suffers afflictions, pain, toil, calamity, or provocation without murmuring or complaining.

~Kindness~

Kindness is the act of good will or benevolence which delights in contributing to the happiness of others. This action is exercised cheerfully in gratifying the wishes of others. Kindness ever accompanies love.

~Goodness~

Goodness is basically the state of being good. Goodness involves benevolence, compassion, or mercy.

~Faithfulness~

Faithfulness is fidelity or loyalty to promises, vows, or covenants. It is being an honest man or woman of your word.

~Gentleness~

Gentleness is having softness of manners, a mild temper, or meekness. It's similar to being tender-hearted.

~Self-Control~

Self-control is the ability to control our emotions and desires, especially in difficult situations.

It is only by the Holy Spirit that we are going to be able to perform pure acts of love and the will of our Father in heaven. I often pray that the Holy Spirit will guide me, flow through me, and direct my path in life. Again, the Holy Spirit is our Advocate, Helper, and Comforter. He teaches us and speaks to us by His still small voice, visions and dreams, the word of God, or through others. He is our conscience and convicts us when necessary.

Our hearts and minds need to be open, and we need to listen carefully to what He has to say. Remember, the Holy Spirit is not just the Spirit

Himself. He is God the Father, Jesus Christ, and the Holy Spirit all in one. When God speaks to us, so are Jesus and the Holy Spirit. When Jesus speaks to us, so are God and the Spirit. When the Spirit speaks to us, so are Jesus and the Father.

From the time I was a young child, I was taught to listen to my conscience. But as I grew older I finally realized this biblical truth. It became manifest to me that it wasn't just my conscience but it was the voice of God, the voice of Jesus, and the voice of the Holy Spirit. Don't get me wrong, I am a sinner, and I still fall short of the glory of God even today, but there were times in my life where my "spiritual ears" were deaf due to my choices of living in the flesh and sin. I also couldn't hear the voice of God because I wasn't paying attention to Him through prayer and meditation. I was also lacking in faith.

We need not beat ourselves up because of mistakes we have made in the past. Remember what Jesus said on the cross just before He gave up the ghost, "Forgive them, for they do not know what they are doing" (Luke 23:34). Even true believers in Christ can be wrong at times, maybe many times. In Proverbs 14:12, it says, "There is a way that appears to be right, but in the end it leads to death."

I've prayed to the Father at times, forgive *us* because *we* do not know what we do.

Romans 7:14-17 states, "We know that the law is spiritual; but I am unspiritual, sold as a slave to sin. I do not understand what I do. For what I want to do I do not do, but what I hate I do. And if I do what I do not want to do, I agree that the law is good. As it is, it is no longer I myself who do it, but it is sin living in me."

God the Father, Jesus, and the Holy Spirit will show us the changes that need to take place in our hearts through conviction. Remember, we are in the process of being conformed to the image and likeness of Jesus. His love, His personality, His character, His actions, His speech, and all of His attributes are being molded and shaped in us. It's a long process. I'm not the same believer today that I was thirty years ago, and should I live thirty more years, only God knows what I will be like then, because He is the potter and we are the clay. He is the refiner of the heart, burning away the impurities so that He can have that intimate personal relationship with us and help us to love others on a much deeper level.

CHAPTER FOUR

Water Baptism

Whoever believes and is baptized will be saved, but whoever does not believe will be condemned. (Mark 16:16)

For we were all baptized by one Spirit so as to form one body—whether Jews or Gentiles, slave or free—and we were all given the one Spirit to drink. (1 Corinthians 12:13)

And this water symbolizes baptism that now saves you also—not the removal of dirt from the body but the pledge of a clear conscience toward God. It saves you by the resurrection of Jesus Christ. (1 Peter 3:21)

So he ordered that they be baptized in the name of Jesus Christ. Then they asked Peter to stay with them for a few days. (Acts 10:48)

And now what are you waiting for? Get up, be baptized and wash your sins away, calling on His name. (Acts 22:16)

Having been buried with Him in baptism, in which you were also raised with Him through your faith in the working of God, who raised Him from the dead. (Colossians 2:12)

For all of you who were baptized into Christ have clothed yourselves with Christ. (Galatians 3:27)

Therefore go and make disciples of all nations, baptizing them in the name of the Father and of the Son and of the

Holy Spirit, and teaching them to obey everything I have commanded you. And surely I am with you always, to the very end of the age." (Matthew 28:19-20)

They replied, "Believe in the Lord Jesus, and you will be saved—you and your household." Then they spoke the word of the Lord to him and to all the others in his house. At that hour of the night the jailer took them and washed their wounds; then immediately he and all his household were baptized. (Acts 16:31-33)

Or don't you know that all of us who were baptized into Christ Jesus were baptized into His death? We were therefore buried with Him through baptism into death in order that, just as Christ was raised from the dead through the glory of the Father, we too may live a new life. For if we have been united with Him in a death like His, we will certainly also be united with Him in a resurrection like His. For we know that our old self was crucified with Him so that the body ruled by sin might be done away with, that we should no longer be slaves to sin—because anyone who has died has been set free from sin. (Romans 6:3-7)

Now if we died with Christ, we believe that we will also live with Him. For we know that since Christ was raised from the dead, He cannot die again; death no longer has mastery over Him. The death He died, He died to sin once for all; but the life He lives, He lives to God. In the same way, count yourselves dead to sin but alive to God in Christ Jesus. Therefore do not let sin reign in your mortal body so that you obey its evil desires. Do not offer any part of yourself to sin as an instrument of wickedness, but rather offer yourselves to God as those who have been brought from death to life; and offer every part of yourself to Him as an instrument of righteousness. (Romans 6:8-13)

For sin shall no longer be your master, because you are not under the law, but under grace. What then? Shall we sin because we are not under the law but under grace? By no means! Don't you know that when you offer yourselves to someone as obedient slaves, you are slaves of the one you obey—whether you are slaves to sin, which leads to death, or to obedience, which leads to righteousness? But thanks be to God that, though you used to be slaves to sin, you have come to obey from your heart the pattern of teaching that has now claimed your allegiance. You have been set free from sin and have become slaves to righteousness. (Romans 6:14-18)

Water baptism is very important. It symbolizes the death of the old self and the birth of our new life in Christ. I believe it can be done in private or public to be official. Some people have only been baptized by water once; some have been baptized multiple times. I know for myself, water was sprinkled on my head when I was a child, then I was baptized privately at the age of seventeen which was very meaningful to me. Later on in adulthood, I decided to be baptized publicly at the beach by one of the elders at my church.

Our faith plays a major role in baptism. Remember, without faith it is impossible to please God. I'll be honest with you, there have been many times that I've taken a shower and have asked God in faith to baptize me and wash me clean. The bible says, "unless you change and become as little children, you will never enter the kingdom of heaven" (Matthew 18:3). I have always had a child-like faith in Jesus Christ during the time I have believed in Him, and I hope I never lose that character trait. I am forty-six years old but still feel like I'm in my twenties, just not physically.

The first important step of salvation is that you "declare with your mouth, 'Jesus is Lord,' and believe in your heart that God raised Him from the dead" (Romans 10:9). The second step of obedience after you believe is being baptized. All you need is to be baptized once. I suggest following the example of our Savior Himself. The next two verses explain that Jesus was praying and "went up" out of the water:

> When all the people were being baptized, Jesus was baptized too. And as He was praying, heaven was opened and the Holy Spirit ascended on Him in bodily form like a dove. And a voice came from heaven: "You are my Son, whom I love; with you I am well pleased." (Luke 3:21-22)

> As soon as Jesus was baptized, He went up out of the water. At that moment heaven was opened, and He saw the Spirit of God descending like a dove and alighting on Him. And a voice from heaven said, "This is my Son, whom I love; with Him I am well pleased." (Matthew 3:16-17)

Maybe every time God's children get baptized, God says that very same thing but we are not aware of it. "This is my son (or daughter), whom I love; with him (or her) I am well pleased." Here are some verses related to being a child of the Most High:

> So in Christ Jesus you are all children of God through faith, for all of you who were baptized into Christ have clothed

yourselves with Christ. (Galatians 3:26-27)

I will be a Father to you, and you will be my sons and daughters, says the Lord Almighty. (2 Corinthians 6:18)

For those who are led by the Spirit of God are the children of God. (Romans 8:14)

So you are no longer a slave, but God's child; and since you are His child, God has made you also an heir. (Galatians 4:7)

Yet to all who did receive Him, to those who believed in His name, He gave the right to become children of God. (John 1:12)

This is how we know who the children of God are and who the children of the devil are: Anyone who does not do what is right is not God's child, nor is anyone who does not love their brother and sister. (1 John 3:10)

CHAPTER FIVE

Holy Spirit and Fire Baptism

~Baptism of the Holy Spirit~

John [the Baptist] answered them all, "I baptize you with water. But one who is more powerful than I will come, the straps of whose sandals I am not worthy to untie. He will baptize you with the Holy Spirit and fire." (Luke 3:16)

And I myself did not know him, but the one who sent me to baptize with water told me, "The man on whom you see the Spirit come down and remain is the one who will baptize with the Holy Spirit." (John 1:33)

And I will ask the Father, and He will give you another advocate to help you and be with you forever—the Spirit of truth. The world cannot accept Him, because it neither sees Him nor knows Him. But you know Him, for He lives with you and will be in you. (John 14:16-17)

Again Jesus said, "Peace be with you! As the Father has sent me, I am sending you." And with that He breathed on them and said, "Receive the Holy Spirit." (John 20:21-22)

On one occasion while He was eating with them [the apostles He had chosen], He gave them this command: "Do not leave Jerusalem, but wait for the gift my

Father promised, which you have heard me speak about. For John baptized with water, but in a few days you will be baptized with the Holy Spirit." (Acts 1:4-5)

But you will receive power when the Holy Spirit comes on you; and you will be my witnesses in Jerusalem, and in all Judea and Samaria, and to the ends of the earth." (Acts 1:8)

When the day of Pentecost came, they were all together in one place. Suddenly a sound like the blowing of a violent wind came from heaven and filled the whole house where they were sitting. They saw what seemed to be tongues of fire that separated and came to rest on each of them. All of them were filled with the Holy Spirit and began to speak in other tongues as the Spirit enabled them. (Acts 2:1-4)

Then Peter stood up with the Eleven, raised his voice and addressed the crowd: "Fellow Jews and all of you who live in Jerusalem, let me explain this to you; listen carefully to what I say. These people are not drunk, as you suppose. It's only nine in the morning! No, this is what was spoken by the prophet Joel: "In the last days, God says, I will pour out my Spirit on all people. Your sons and daughters will prophesy, your young men will see visions, your old men will dream dreams. Even on my servants, both men and women, I will pour out my Spirit in those days, and they will prophesy. I will show wonders in the heavens above and signs on the earth below, blood and fire and billows of smoke. The sun will be turned to darkness and the moon to blood before the coming of the great and glorious day of the Lord. And everyone who calls on the name of the Lord will be saved." (Acts 2:14-21)

Notice, when the apostles were filled with the Holy Spirit they began to speak in other tongues. Speaking in tongues is a spiritual gift from God, and I don't believe you necessarily have to receive that gift to obtain the Holy Spirit. In fact, the bible says, "where there are prophesies, they will cease; where there are tongues, they will be stilled; where there is knowledge, it will pass away. For we know in part and we prophesy in part, but when completeness comes, what is in part disappears" (1 Corinthians 13:8-10).

~Baptism of Fire~

> I baptize you with water for repentance. But after me comes one who is more powerful than I, whose sandals I am not worthy to carry. He will baptize you with the Holy Spirit and fire. His winnowing fork is in His hand, and He will clear His threshing floor, gathering His wheat into the barn and burning up the chaff with unquenchable fire. (Matthew 3:11-12)

From my studies, I have learned that the baptism of Holy Spirit and fire are not separate but go hand in hand. As you saw from the excerpt from the book of Acts, it said that tongues of fire rested upon them when they received the Holy Spirit.

Other than that, the bible doesn't go into much detail about the fire that is associated with the baptism of the Holy Spirit.

I believe the fire it talks about is unique for each individual. I first felt that I was being baptized by fire when I felt strong conviction and the fear of the Lord. The bible says, "our God is a consuming fire" (Hebrews 12:29), and "the fear of the Lord is the beginning of wisdom" (Proverbs 9:10). So at first, it was fear to me, and then I received some wisdom after repentance. Then I felt that fire by hearing His voice in meditation and prayer saying, "I'm baptizing you in fire," and at that time, it was peaceful.

I confidently believe that if you declare with your mouth, "Jesus is Lord," and believe in your heart that God raised Him from the dead, you will be saved and Jesus will give you the Holy Spirit. The eternal fire spoken of in the book of Revelation is what I feared the most. I remember a time when I was about thirty-five years old that I was reading Matthew 7:23 which says, "I never knew you; depart from Me, you who practice lawlessness!" I took it personally and wept in fear of the Lord and begged Him not to send me to hell. I was feeling very strong conviction at the time. It amazes me how people just brush off the topic of eternal fire, and "there is no fear of God before their eyes" (Romans 3:18).

So, I think the Holy Spirit can make us uncomfortable because God is convicting us and trying to change our heart while other times He can comfort us with the peace that transcends all understanding (Philippians 4:7). I believe the baptism of fire spoken of by John the Baptist is where Jesus burns the impurities in our hearts and lights a fire in us to take up our cross and follow Him. Jesus said, "Blessed are the pure in heart, for they will see God" (Matthew 5:8).

CHAPTER SIX

Being Born Again

Now there was a Pharisee, a man named Nicodemus who was a member of the Jewish ruling council. He came to Jesus at night and said, "Rabbi, we know that you are a teacher who has come from God. For no one could perform the signs you are doing if God were not with Him."

Jesus replied, "Very truly I tell you, no one can see the kingdom of God unless they are born again.

"How can someone be born when they are old?" Nicodemus asked. "Surely they cannot enter a second time into their mother's womb to be born!"

Jesus answered, "Very truly I tell you, no one can enter the kingdom of God unless they are born of water and the Spirit. Flesh gives birth to flesh, but the Spirit gives birth to spirit. You should not be surprised at my saying, 'You must be born again.' The wind blows wherever it pleases. You hear its sound, but you cannot tell where it comes from or where it is going. So it is with everyone born of the Spirit."

"How can this be?" Nicodemus asked.

"You are Israel's teacher," said Jesus, "and do you not understand these things?" (John 3:1-10)

Praise be to the God and Father of our Lord Jesus Christ! In His great mercy He has given us new birth into a living hope through the resurrection of Jesus Christ from the dead, and into an inheritance that can never perish, spoil or fade. This inheritance is kept in heaven for you, who through faith are shielded by God's power until the coming of the salvation that is ready to be revealed in the last time. (1 Peter 1:3-5)

So from now on we regard no one from a worldly point of view. Though we once regarded Christ in this way, we do so no longer. Therefore, if anyone is in Christ, the new creation has come: The old has gone, the new is here! All this is from God, who reconciled us to Himself through Christ and gave us the ministry of reconciliation: that God was reconciling the world to Himself in Christ, not counting people's sins against them. And he has committed to us the message of reconciliation. We are therefore Christ's ambassadors, as though God were making His appeal through us. We implore you on Christ's behalf: Be reconciled to God. God made

Him who had no sin to be sin for us, so that in Him we might become the righteousness of God. (2 Corinthians 5:16-21)

Now that you have purified yourselves <u>by obeying the truth</u> so that you have sincere love for each other, love one another deeply, from the heart. <u>For you have been born again</u>, not of perishable seed, but of imperishable, through the living and enduring word of God. (1 Peter 1:22-23)

We were therefore buried with Him through baptism into death in order that, just as Christ was raised from the dead through the glory of the Father, we too may live a new life. (Romans 6:4)

The true light that gives light to everyone was coming into the world. He was in the world, and though the world was made through Him, the world did not recognize Him. He came to that which was His own, but His own did not receive Him. <u>Yet to all who did receive Him, to those who believed in His name, He gave the right to become children of God—children born not of natural descent, nor of human decision or a husband's will, but born of God.</u> (John 1:9-13)

Since, then, you have been raised with Christ, set your hearts on things above, where Christ is, seated at the right hand of God. Set your minds on things above, not on earthly things. For you died, and your life is now hidden with Christ in God. When Christ, who is your life, appears, then you also will appear with Him in glory. Put to death, therefore, whatever belongs to your earthly nature; sexual immorality, impurity, lust, evil desires and greed, which is idolatry. Because of these, the wrath of God is coming. You used to walk in these ways, in the life you once lived. But now you must also rid yourselves of all such things as these: anger, rage, malice, slander, and filthy language from your lips. Do not lie to each other, since you have taken off you old self with its practices and have put on the new self, which is being renewed in knowledge in the image of its Creator. (Colossians 3:1-10)

But about the resurrection of the dead—have you not read what God said to you, "I am the God of Abraham, the God of Isaac, and the God of Jacob?" He is not the God of the dead but of the living. (Matthew 22:31-32)

I know for me personally, I do not believe I was born again when I first believed in Jesus Christ and when I was baptized at the age of seventeen. As I said, I became a believer in Christ at the age of fifteen and was baptized in water when I was seventeen but I lived many years not attempting to do the will of my Father in heaven. I lived by the flesh, not the Spirit. I had not put to death my life which belonged to my earthly nature. I lived a life of self-will, desiring things of the world. I would go out and party with others and think to myself, "Jesus sat with sinners." But Jesus was sinless. He had self-control. I'm sure He may have drank wine but not to the point of being a drunkard. I was getting drunk and high on drugs and living a careless, sinful life. The kingdom of God and His righteousness was not first priority in my life until I reached the age of forty-four.

I may have believed in Jesus, but I was not being obedient to His word. I just figured I was free and could live my life however I wanted and didn't consider the consequences. I didn't have reverence for God. I picked out some of His words to live by, but if there was something in the bible that went against my way of life, I would just ignore it. I later learned that the choices I was making and the life I was living was not pleasing to God and those who were close to me. I was basically "lukewarm" and God definitely spit me out of His mouth (Revelation 3:16).

John 3:5 says, "No one can enter the kingdom of God unless they are born of water and of Spirit." It wasn't until after I completely surrendered to God that I believe I was born again. I had just gotten out of jail and I admitted myself voluntarily into a faith-based residential rehab. There were five other clients in our small two bedroom apartment and I began to go into the bathroom and pray to the Father in secret.

One time while I was on my knees praying, I heard that still, small voice saying, "Get in the tub because now I am going to baptize you and you are going to be born again this day." The voice also said, "All your sins are going to be forgotten and I will remember them no more." By faith I believe I was truly born again that day and I'll never forget the experience.

Since I've been born again, I've had a closer relationship with my Father in heaven. I know that He is transforming me into the son He wants me to be. I pray to Him daily and give thanks more than ever because of His blessings on my life. He knows that the time I am spending writing this book is all for His glory. The experience of being born again, I believe, is different and unique for every believer. I just know that for me, I'll never forget the day it happened and I have been receiving blessing after blessing ever since.

CHAPTER SEVEN

Predestination

Before I formed you in the womb I knew you, before you were born I set you apart; I appointed you as a prophet to the nations. (Jeremiah 1:5)

For you created my inmost being; you knit me together in my mother's womb. I praise you because I am fearfully and wonderfully made; your works are wonderful, I know that full well. My frame was not hidden from you when I was made in the secret place, when I was woven together in the depths of the earth. Your eyes saw my unformed body; all the days ordained for me were written in your book before one of them came to be. How precious to me are your thoughts, God! How vast is the sum of them! Were I to count them, they would outnumber the grains of sand—when I awake, I am still with you. (Psalm 139:13-18)

And we know that in all things God works for the good of those who love Him, who have been called according to His purpose. For those God foreknew He also predestined to be conformed to the image of His son, that He might be the firstborn among many brothers and sisters. And those He predestined, He also called; those He called, He also justified; those He justified, He also glorified. (Romans 8:28-30)

No, we declare God's wisdom, a mystery that has been hidden and that God destined for our glory before time began. (1 Corinthians 2:7)

For He chose us in Him before the creation of the world to be holy and blameless in his sight. In love He predestined us for adoption to sonship through Jesus Christ, in accordance with His pleasure and will—to the praise of His glorious grace, which He has freely given us in the One He loves. (Ephesians 1:4-6)

In Him we were also chosen, having been predestined according to the plan of Him who works out everything in conformity with the purpose of His will, in order that we, who were the first to put our hope in Christ, might be for the praise of His glory. And you also were included in Christ when you heard the message of truth, the gospel of your salvation. <u>When you believed, you were marked in Him with a seal, the promised Holy Spirit, who is a deposit guaranteeing our inheritance until the redemption of those who are God's possession—to the praise of His glory.</u> (Ephesians 1:11-14; emphasis

added) (This Scripture declares that
God gave us the Holy Spirit upon believing in Jesus Christ.)

Predestinate is defined as to predetermine or
foreordain; to appoint or ordain beforehand by an
unchangeable purpose.

God is omniscient and omnipotent. He knows
the motives and intentions of our hearts and actions. He knows the stories of our whole lives before they even come to pass. Jesus Christ is our
shepherd, and His sheep were predestined to follow Him before they were even born.

Jesus said, "Enter through the narrow gate. For
wide is the gate and broad is the road that leads to
destruction, and many enter through it. But small
is the gate and narrow the road that leads to life
and only a few find it" (Matthew 7:13-14).

This faith and belief is a gift from God. I believe
many of those who continually reject Christ are
basically children of the wicked one. After Eve ate
of the forbidden fruit in the garden, God declared
to the serpent, "I will put enmity between you and
the woman, and between your offspring and hers"
(Genesis 3:15).

Jesus spoke a parable about a man who sowed good seed in his field, which describes the children of God and the children of the wicked one:

> The kingdom of heaven is like a man who sowed good seed in his field. But while everyone was sleeping, his enemy sowed weeds among the wheat [Children of God's seed and children of the devil's seed].... So the servants wanted to pull the weeds but the man said let them grow together until the harvest. Upon harvest, we will gather the weeds and burn them, then gather the wheat and bring it into my barn. (Matthew 13:24-30; paraphrase)

> For it is by grace you have been saved, through faith—and this is not from yourselves, it is the gift of God—not by works, so that no one can boast. For we are God's handiwork, created in Christ Jesus to do good works, which God prepared in advance for us to do. (Ephesians 2:8-10)

In Romans 8:29 it says, "For those He foreknew he also predestined to be conformed to the image of His son..." God had previous knowledge of and foreknew those who would believe in Jesus Christ. He has a plan for our lives in which others may glorify Him through us. He knows everything about us that happened in our past, everything that will happen today, and everything that will happen in the future. As I said before, He is the potter, and we are the clay. His work is to conform us to the image and likeness of His Son, Jesus. He is doing the work, we are not. Jesus said, "The work of God is this: to believe in the one He has sent" (John 6:29).

"All of us have become like one who is unclean, and all our righteous acts are like filthy rags; we all shrivel up like a leaf, and like the wind our sins sweep us away" (Isaiah 64:6). Jesus said, "I am the vine; you are the branches. If you remain in Me and I in you, you will bear much fruit; apart from Me you can do nothing" (John 15:5). This is so true. I would not be where I am today if it wasn't for God the Father, Jesus Christ, and the Holy Spirit.

We were predestined to love our Father, Jesus, and the Holy Spirit. We were predestined to love our neighbors, enemies, and ourselves. We were predestined to love as defined in 1 Corinthians 13.

We were predestined to love as Jesus loved. We were predestined to live in God and to have God live in us. We were predestined to see miracles take place in our lives as well as in the lives of others. We were predestined to witness healing and restoration in our lives and in the lives of others. We need to thank God often and give all glory to Him, His Son, and the Holy Spirit.

CHAPTER EIGHT

Our Unique Calling

You did not choose me, but I chose you and appointed you so that you might go and bear fruit—fruit that will last—and so that whatever you ask in my name the Father will give you. This is my command: Love each other. (John 15:16-17)

And we know that in all things God works for the good of those who love

Him, who have been called according to His purpose. (Romans 8:28)

The one who calls you is faithful, and He will do it. (1 Thessalonians 5:24)

I press toward the goal to win the prize for which God has called me heavenward in Christ Jesus. (Philippians 3:14)

He called you to this through our gospel, that you might share in the glory of our Lord Jesus Christ. (2 Thessalonians 2:14)

He has saved us and called us to a holy life—not because of anything we have done but because of His own purpose and grace. This grace was given us in Christ Jesus before the beginning of time. (2 Timothy 1:9) (Predestination and Calling)

To this you were called, because Christ suffered for you, leaving you an example, that you should follow in His steps. (1 Peter 2:21)

There is one body and one Spirit, just as you were called to one hope when you were called. (Ephesians 4:4)

But just as He who called you is holy, so be holy in all you do; for it is written: "Be holy, because I am holy." (1 Peter 1:15-16)

Do not repay evil with evil or insult with insult. On the contrary, repay evil with blessing, because to this you were called so that you may inherit a blessing. (1 Peter 3:9)

God is faithful, who has called you into fellowship with His Son, Jesus Christ our Lord. (1 Corinthians 1:9)

Everyone who believes in Jesus Christ as their Lord and savior has special gifts from God and a unique calling on their lives:

Each of you should use whatever gift you have received to serve others, as faithful stewards of God's grace in its various forms. If anyone speaks, they should do so as one who speaks the very words of God. If anyone serves, they should do so with the strength God provides, so that in all things God may be praised through Jesus Christ. To Him be the glory and the power forever and ever. Amen. (1 Peter 4:10-11)

For just as each of us has one body with many members, and these members do not all have the same function, so in Christ we, though many, form one body, and each member belongs to all the others. We have different gifts, according to the grace given to each of us. If your gift is prophesying, then prophesy in accordance with your faith; if it is serving, then serve; if it is teaching, then teach; if it is to encourage, then give encouragement; if it is giving, then give generously; if it is to lead, do it diligently; if it is to show mercy, do it cheerfully. (Romans 12:4-8)

Nevertheless, each person should live as a believer in whatever situation the Lord has assigned to them, just as God has called them. (1 Corinthians 7:17)

I would like you to be free from concern. An unmarried man is concerned about the Lord's affairs—how he can please the Lord. But a married man is concerned about the affairs of this world—how he can please his wife—and his interests are divided. An unmarried woman or virgin is concerned about the Lord's affairs: Her aim is to be devoted to the Lord in both body and spirit. But a married woman is concerned about the affairs of this world—how she can please her husband. (1 Corinthians 7:32-34)

So Christ Himself gave the apostles, the prophets, the evangelists, the pastors and teachers, to equip His people for works of service, so that the body of Christ may be built up until we all reach unity in the faith and in the knowledge of the Son of God and become mature, attaining to the whole measure of the fullness of Christ. (Ephesians 4:11-13)

There are different kinds of gifts, but the same Spirit distributes them. There are different kinds of service, but the same Lord. There are different kinds of working, but in all of them and in everyone it is the same God at work. Now to each one the manifestation of the Spirit is given for the common good. To one there is given through the Spirit a message of wisdom, to another a message of knowledge by means of the same Spirit, to another faith by the same Spirit, to another, gifts of healing by that one Spirit, to another, miraculous powers, to another prophecy, to another distinguishing between spirits, to another speaking in different kinds of tongues. (1 Corinthians 12:4-10)

And God has placed in the church first of all apostles, second prophets, third teachers, then miracles, then gifts of healing, of helping, of guidance, and of different kinds of tongues. (1 Corinthians 12:28)

Now eagerly desire the greater gifts. And yet I will show you the most excellent way. (1 Corinthians 12:31)

Follow the way of love and eagerly desire gifts of the Spirit, especially prophecy. (1 Corinthians 14:1)

But the one who prophesies speaks to people for their strengthening, encouraging and comfort. (1 Corinthians 14:3)

The spirits of prophets are subject to the control of prophets. For God is not a God of disorder but of peace—as in all the congregation of the Lord's people. (1 Corinthians 14:32-33)

God gave all those who believe in Jesus Christ gifts. You can find them in Romans 12 and 1 Corinthians 12. It is important for us to find out what our strongest gift is so we can serve the body of Christ and use that gift for the furthering of the gospel and the kingdom. Jesus said, "Ask and it will be given to you; seek and you will find; knock and the door will be opened to you" (Matthew 7:7). For so long I was oblivious to my gift but one day it was finally revealed to me. For many years I have been trying to encourage my friends on Facebook by posting scriptures, images with verses on them and YouTube Christian music videos. Most of my posts have been related to Christ and the bible.

I have always thought of myself as having the gift of helping because I have tried to help others when necessary but there was much more to my gift. The New King James Version of the bible writes about the gift of exhortation but for so long I didn't look into it because I didn't know that it meant to encourage. But I finally realized that my strongest gift is and has been exhortation or encouragement. Now that I know what my strongest spiritual gift is, I just want to take the ball and run with it by sharing the hope and comfort of Jesus Christ.

CHAPTER NINE

Justification by Faith

Therefore no one will be declared righteous in God's sight by the works of the law; rather, through the law we become conscious of our sin. But now apart from the law the righteousness of God has been made known, to which the Law and the Prophets testify. This righteousness is given through faith in Jesus Christ to all who believe. There is no difference between Jew and Gentile, for all have sinned and fall short of the glory of God, and all are justified freely by His grace through the redemption that came by Christ Jesus. (Romans 3:20-24)

Therefore, since we have been justified through faith, we have peace with God through our Lord Jesus Christ, through whom we have gained access by faith into this grace in which we now stand. (Romans 5:1-2)

Since we have now been justified by His blood, how much more shall we be saved from God's wrath through Him! (Romans 5:9)

What, then, shall we say in response to these things? If God is for us, who can be against us? He who did not spare His own Son, but gave Him up for us all—how will He not also, along with Him, graciously give us all things? Who will bring any charge against those whom God has chosen? It is God who justifies. Who then is the one who condemns?

No one. Christ Jesus who died—more than that, who was raised to life—is at the right hand of God and is also interceding for us. (Romans 8:31-34)

At one time we too were foolish, disobedient, deceived and enslaved by all kinds of passions and pleasures. We lived in malice and envy, being hated and hating one another. But when the kindness and love of God our Savior appeared, He saved us, not because of righteous things we had done, but because of His mercy. He saved us through the washing of rebirth and renewal by the Holy Spirit, whom He poured out on us generously through Jesus Christ our Savior, so that, having been justified by His grace, we might become heirs having the hope of eternal life. This is a trustworthy saying. And I want you to stress these things, so that those who have trusted in God may be careful to devote themselves to doing what is good. These things are excellent and profitable for everyone. (Titus 3:3-8)

In theology, justification is defined as remission of sin and absolution from guilt and punishment or an act of free grace by which God pardons the sinner and accepts him as righteous, on account of the atonement of Jesus Christ.

Our belief in Jesus Christ puts us in a right standing before God, and He adopts us as His children. Jesus said, "I am the way and the truth and the life. No one comes to the Father except through Me" (John 14:6). This adoption is described in detail:

> For those who are led by the Spirit of God are the children of God. The Spirit you received does not make you slaves, so that you live in fear again; rather, the Spirit you received brought about your adoption to sonship. And by Him we cry, "Abba, Father." The Spirit Himself testifies with our spirit that we are God's children. Now if God's children, then we are heirs—heirs of God and co-heirs with Christ, if indeed we share in His sufferings in order that we may also share in His glory. (Romans 8:14-17)

Have you shared in Christ's sufferings? I believe many of us have. Remember Romans 8:18, "I consider that our present sufferings are not worth comparing with the glory that will be revealed in us."

> Those who sow with tears will reap with songs of joy. Those who go out weeping, carrying seed to sow, will return with songs of joy, carrying sheaves with them. (Psalm 126:5-6)

> Blessed are those who mourn, for they will be comforted. (Matthew 5:4)

~Verses about Faith~

> Who is it that overcomes the world? Only the one who believes that Jesus is the Son of God. (1 John 5:5)

> I have been crucified with Christ and I no longer live, but Christ lives in me. The life I now live in the body, I live by faith in the Son of God, who loved me and gave Himself for me. (Galatians 2:20)

The Son is the radiance of God's glory and the exact representation of His being, sustaining all things by His powerful word. After He had provided purification for sins, He sat down at the right hand of the Majesty in heaven. (Hebrews 1:3)

But when you ask, you must believe and not doubt, because the one who doubts is like a wave of the sea, blown and tossed by the wind. (James 1:6)

"Go," said Jesus, "your faith has healed you." Immediately he received his sight and followed Jesus along the road. (Mark 10:52)

For in the gospel the righteousness of God is revealed—a righteousness that is by faith from first to last, just as it is written: "The righteous will live by faith." (Romans 1:17)

For it is with your heart that you believe and are justified, and it is with your mouth that you profess your faith and are saved. (Romans 10:10)

Now faith is confidence in what we hope for and assurance about what we do not see. (Hebrews 11:1)

Through Him you believe in God, who raised Him from the dead and glorified Him, and so your faith and hope are in God. (1 Peter 1:21)

In all this you greatly rejoice, though now for a little while you may have had to suffer grief in all kinds of trials. These have come so that the proven genuineness of your faith—of greater worth than gold, which perishes even though refined by fire—may result in praise, glory and honor when Jesus Christ is revealed. (1 Peter 1:6-7)

For we live by faith, not by sight. (2 Corinthians 5:7)

Be on your guard; stand firm in the faith; be courageous; be strong. (1 Corinthians 16:13)

I have fought the good fight, I have finished the race, I have kept the faith. (2 Timothy 4:7)

In addition to all this, take up the shield of faith, with which you can extinguish all the flaming arrows of the evil one. (Ephesians 6:16)

For through the Spirit we eagerly await by faith the righteousness for which we hope. (Galatians 5:5)

Let us draw near to God with a sincere heart and with the full assurance that faith brings, having our hearts sprinkled to cleanse us from a guilty conscience and having our bodies washed with pure water. (Hebrews 10:22)

The testing of your faith produces perseverance. (James 1:3)

Consequently, faith comes from hearing the message, and the message is heard through the word about Christ. (Romans 10:17)

CHAPTER TEN

Sufferings

But even if you should suffer for what is right, you are blessed. "Do not fear their threats; do not be frightened." (1 Peter 3:14)

Therefore, since Christ suffered in His body, arm yourselves also with the same attitude, because whoever suffers in the body is done with sin. (1 Peter 4:1)

And the God of all grace, who called you to His eternal glory in Christ, after you have suffered a little while, will Himself restore you and make you strong, firm and steadfast. (1 Peter 5:10)

For our light and momentary troubles are achieving for us an eternal glory that far outweighs them all. (2 Corinthians 4:17)

In fact, everyone who wants to live a godly life in Christ Jesus will be persecuted. (2 Timothy 3:12)

Now I rejoice in what I am suffering for you, and I fill up in my flesh what is still lacking in regard to Christ's afflictions, for the sake of His body, which is the church. (Colossians 1:24)

Carry each other's burdens, and in this way you will fulfill the law of Christ. (Galatians 6:2)

In bringing many sons and daughters to glory, it was fitting that God, for whom and through whom everything exists, should make the pioneer of their salvation perfect through what He suffered. (Hebrews 2:10)

He was despised and rejected by mankind, a man of suffering, and familiar with pain. Like one from whom people hide their faces He was despised, and we held Him in low esteem. (Isaiah 53:3)

Blessed is the one who perseveres under trial because, having stood the test, that person will receive the crown of life that the Lord has promised to those who love Him. (James 1:12)

I want to know Christ—yes, to know the power of His resurrection and participation in His sufferings, becoming like Him in His death. (Philippians 3:10)

It was good for me to be afflicted so that I might learn your decrees. (Psalm 119:71)

Not only so, but we also glory in our sufferings, because we know that suffering produces perseverance; perseverance, character; and character, hope. (Romans 5:3-4)

But rejoice inasmuch as you participate in the sufferings of Christ, so that you may be overjoyed when His glory is revealed. (1 Peter 4:13)

For it is commendable if someone bears up under the pain of unjust suffering because they are conscious of God. But how is it to your credit if you receive a beating for doing wrong and endure it? But if you suffer for doing good and you endure it, this is commendable before God. To this you were called, because Christ suffered for you, leaving you an example, that you should follow in His steps. (1 Peter 2:19-21)

We are hard pressed on every side, but not crushed; perplexed, but not in despair; persecuted, but not abandoned;

struck down, but not destroyed. We always carry around in our body the death of Jesus, so that the life of Jesus may also be revealed in our body. (2 Corinthians 4:8-10)

Consider it pure joy, my brothers and sisters, whenever you face trials of many kinds, because you know that the testing of your faith produces perseverance. Let perseverance finish its work so that you may be mature and complete, not lacking anything. (James 1:2-4)

Blessed are you when people insult you, persecute you and falsely say all kinds of evil against you because of me. Rejoice and be glad, because great is your reward in heaven, for in the same way they persecuted the prophets who were before you. (Matthew 5:11-12)

Rejoice always, pray continually, and give thanks in all circumstances; for

this is God's will for you in Christ Jesus.
(1 Thessalonians 5:16-18)

I believe sufferings bring us closer to God. The bible says, "The Lord is close to the brokenhearted and saves those who are crushed in spirit" (Psalm 34:18). When things seem to be going well in life, we may have a tendency to put God on the back burner and are occupied with other things that distract us from Him. After suffering a little (or a lot) we may be more thankful for the good times and the blessings He bestows upon us. I also believe that through sufferings, God is trying to get our attention. It's kind of like a man who is living in sin and breaking the law. He's fine until he finally gets caught and ends up in jail or prison. It's not until his freedom gets taken away that he cries out to God, "Please help me get out of this, and I will stop doing the things I have been doing!" Some people take heed to discipline early in life, while for others it may take longer, and some maybe never accept the fact that they need to change, thereby continuing to live a life of turmoil.

If you are suffering today and have suffered a lot in the past, I encourage you to remember there is a light at the end of the tunnel. That light is Jesus

Christ. He is the deliverer. He is the God of restoration. He is our miraculous healer. I urge you not to harden your hearts. Confide in other believers you can trust and confess your sins to; so that you may be healed. You'll know which ones you can trust. Jesus said, "Watch out for false prophets. They come to you in sheep's clothing, but inwardly they are ferocious wolves. By their fruit you will recognize them" (Matthew 7:15-16). "A good tree cannot bear bad fruit, and a bad tree cannot bear good fruit" (Matthew 7:18). We all have burdens that we are supposed to help each other with. Jesus will put the right people in your life who will share their faith and hope with you and love you wherever you are at in your walk with Him.

CHAPTER ELEVEN

Glory (God's and Ours)

~God's Glory~

The heavens declare the glory of God; the skies proclaim the work of His hands. (Psalm 19:1)

And there were shepherds living out in the fields nearby, keeping watch over their flocks at night. An angel of the Lord appeared to them, and the glory of the Lord shone around them, and they were terrified. But the angel said to them, "Do not be afraid. I bring you good news that will cause great joy for all the people. Today in the town of David a Savior has been born to you; He is the Messiah, the Lord. This will be a sign to you: You will find a baby wrapped in cloths and lying in a manger." Suddenly a great company of the heavenly host appeared with the angel, praising God and saying, "Glory to God in the highest heaven, and on earth peace to those on whom His favor rests." (Luke 2:8-14)

The Word became flesh and made His dwelling among us. We have seen His glory, the glory of the one and only Son, who came from the Father, full of grace and truth. (John 1:14)

Against all hope, Abraham in hope believed and so became the father of many nations, just as it had been said to him, "So shall your offspring be."

Without weakening in his faith, he faced the fact that his body was as good as dead—since he was about a hundred years old—and that Sarah's womb was also dead. Yet he did not waver through unbelief regarding the promise of God, but was strengthened in his faith and gave glory to God, being fully persuaded that God had power to do what He had promised. This is why "it was credited to him as righteousness." (Romans 4:18-22)

So whether you eat or drink or whatever you do, do it all for the glory of God. (1 Corinthians 10:31)

Then Jesus said, "Did I not tell you that if you believe, you will see the glory of God?" (John 11:40)

For God, who said, "Let light shine out of darkness," made His light shine in our hearts to give us the light of the knowledge of God's glory displayed in the face of Christ. (2 Corinthians 4:6)

It is written: "I believed; therefore I have spoken." Since we have that same spirit of faith, we also believe and therefore speak, because we know that the one who raised the Lord Jesus from the dead will also raise us with Jesus and present us with you to Himself. All this is for your benefit, so that the grace that is reaching more and more people may cause thanksgiving to overflow to the glory of God. (2 Corinthians 4:13-15)

For this reason I kneel before the Father, from whom every family in heaven and on earth derives its name. I pray that out of His glorious riches He may strengthen you with power through His Spirit in your inner being, so that Christ may dwell in your hearts through faith. (Ephesians 3:14-16)

Therefore God exalted Him to the highest place and gave Him the name that is above every name, that at the name of Jesus every knee should bow, in heaven and on earth and under the earth, and every tongue acknowledge that Jesus Christ is Lord, to the glory of God the Father. (Philippians 2:9-11)

And my God will meet all your needs according to the riches of His glory in Christ Jesus. To our God and Father be glory forever and ever. Amen. (Philippians 4:19-20)

~Our Glory~

I consider that our present sufferings are not worth comparing with the glory that will be revealed in us. For the creation waits in eager expectation for the children of God to be revealed. For the creation was subjected to frustration, not by its own choice, but by the will of the one who subjected it, in hope that the creation itself will be liberated from its bondage to decay and brought into the freedom and glory of the children of God. (Romans 8:18-21)

I have become [the church's] servant by
the commission God gave me to present to you the word of God in its fullness—the mystery that has been kept
hidden for ages and generations, but is
now disclosed to the Lord's people. To
them God has chosen to make known
among the Gentiles the glorious riches
of this mystery, which is Christ in you,
the hope of glory. (Colossians 1:25-27)

So, not only are we going to see God's glory but
our glory as well. Our glory is first and foremost in
God, Jesus Christ, and the Holy Spirit. For so long
I had read about God's glory but it wasn't until re-
cently that I found out about glory in us also. Just to
be the least in heaven would be glory to me. Romans
talks about the glory that will be revealed in us. I
wonder what that is going to be like. I used to relate
to grief and depression but now I am breaking out
of suffering. I don't know what the future holds.
Only God knows, but I am very excited. Many
blessings have been coming my way, and I pray for
more. All I know is I have to be a faithful steward
of what God has given me today. I'm mostly concerned with God's glory. He deserves it for what He

had to go through. God in the flesh, having no sin, came down to the earth as a humble servant and was beaten, whipped, spit on, mocked, persecuted, and crucified; all for the sins of the world.

I hope I get to see God. I hope my heart is pure. I hope I had done everything I could to yield to His will for my life. I hope I hear the words, "Well done, my son and servant. I love you and I know you. Come on in, your name is in the Lamb's Book of Life."

CHAPTER TWELVE

Sanctification

S anctification is defined as the act of making holy. It's the act of God's grace by which the affections of men are purified or alienated from sin and the world, and exalted to a supreme love of God.

Holy is defined as whole, entire or perfect, in a moral sense. Holy can also mean pure in heart, temper or dispositions free from sin and sinful affections. A man can be called holy when his heart is conformed in some degree to the image of God, and his life is regulated by the divine precepts.

~Prayer of Jesus and His Comment on Sanctification~

I am coming to you now, but I say these things while I am still in the world, so that they may have the full measure of my joy within them. I have given them your word and the world has hated them, for they are not of the world any more than I am of the world. My prayer is not that you take them out of the world but that you protect them from the evil one. They are not of the world, even as I am not of it. Sanctify them by the truth; your word is truth. As you sent Me into the world, I have sent them into the world. For them I sanctify myself, that they too may be truly sanctified. (John 17:13-19)

~Verses about Sanctification~

Or do you not know that wrongdoers will not inherit the kingdom of God? Do not be deceived: Neither the sexually immoral nor idolaters nor adulterers nor men who have sex with men nor thieves nor the greedy nor drunkards nor slanderers nor swindlers will inherit the kingdom of God. And that is what some of you were. But you were washed, you were sanctified, you were justified in the name of the Lord Jesus Christ and by the Spirit of our God. (1 Corinthians 6:9-11)

The high priest carries the blood of animals into the Most Holy Place as a sin offering, but the bodies are burned outside the camp. And so Jesus also suffered outside the city gate to make the people holy through His own blood. (Hebrews 13:11-12)

First He said, "Sacrifices and offerings, burnt offerings and sin offerings you did not desire, nor were you pleased with them"—though they were offered in accordance with the law. Then He said, "Here I am, I have come to do your will." He sets aside the first to establish the second. And by that will, <u>we have</u> <u>been made holy through the sacrifice</u> <u>of the body of Jesus Christ once for all</u>. (Hebrews 10:8-10)

It is God's will that you should be sanctified: that you should avoid sexual immorality; that each of you should learn to control your own body in a way that is holy and honorable, not in passionate lust like the pagans, who do not know God; and that in this matter no one should wrong or take advantage of a brother or sister. The Lord will punish all those who commit such sins, as we told you and warned you before. For God did not call us to be impure, but to live a holy life. (1 Thessalonians 4:3-7)

If we confess our sins, He is faithful and just and will forgive us our sins and purify us from all unrighteousness. (1 John 1:9)

For by one sacrifice He has made perfect forever those who are being made holy. (Hebrews 10:14)

Moreover, we have all had human fathers who disciplined us and we respected them for it. How much more should we submit to the Father of spirits and live! They disciplined us for a little while as they thought best; but God disciplines us for our good, in order that we may share in His holiness. No discipline seems pleasant at the time, but painful. Later on, however, it produces a harvest of righteousness and peace for those who have been trained by it. (Hebrews 12:9-11)

No one who is born of God will continue to sin, because God's seed remains in them; they cannot go on sinning, because they have been born of God. (1 John 3:9)

Have you been born again? Is God's seed in you? If not, pray to the Father about it, and He will direct your path. If you are not born again and you desire to be a new creation, it will happen, and I believe you'll never forget the date. It's like having a second date of birth. It is God's will for His children to be born again. I guarantee you'll never be the same.

The apostle Paul said we were washed, sanctified and justified. He also said we have been made holy through the sacrifice of Christ's body once for all. The bible is expressing these truths in past tense as if sanctification has already taken place in our lives. Most argue that sanctification is a life-long process but what if we are sanctified already by the justification of faith? Didn't Paul clearly state that we are not under the law and that our righteousness comes by faith? Do people seek to be sanctified by their works? Remember the words of Isaiah: "All of us have become like one who is unclean, and all our righteous acts are like filthy rags." (Isaiah 64:6) For me, I just stand firm on the word of God. Maybe when it comes to the subject of sanctification we should remember what Jesus said right before He gave up the ghost on the cross, "It is finished." Our sanctification, I believe, is found in Him.

CHAPTER THIRTEEN

Loving God the Father

Love the Lord your God with all your heart and with all your soul and with all your mind and with all your strength. (Mark 12:30)

Look to the Lord and His strength; seek His face always. (1 Chronicles 16:11)

Now devote your heart and soul to seeking the Lord your God. (1 Chronicles 22:19)

My son, give me your heart and let your eyes delight in my ways, for an adulterous woman is a deep pit, and a wayward wife is a narrow well. (Proverbs 23:26-27)

You will seek me and find me when you seek me with all your heart. (Jeremiah 29:13)

Jesus replied, "Anyone who loves me will obey my teaching. My Father will love them, and we will come to them and make our home with them." (John 14:23)

Do not conform to the pattern of this world, but be transformed by the renewing of your mind. Then you will be able to test and approve what God's will is—His good, pleasing and perfect will. (Romans 12:2)

For in Him all things were created: things in heaven and on earth, visible and invisible, whether thrones or powers or rulers or authorities; all things have been created through Him and for Him. (Colossians 1:16)

Since, then, you have been raised with Christ, set your hearts on things above, where Christ is, seated at the right hand of God. Set your minds on things above, not on earthly things. For you died, and your life is now hidden with Christ in God. When Christ, who is your life, appears, then you also will appear with Him in glory. (Colossians 3:1-4)

Jesus said, "If you love me, keep my commands. And I will ask the Father, and He will give you another advocate to help you and be with you forever—the Spirit of truth. The world cannot accept Him, because it neither sees Him nor knows Him. But you know Him, for He lives with you and will be in you. (John 14:15-17)

You adulterous people, don't you know that friendship with the world means enmity against God? Therefore, anyone who chooses to be a friend of the world becomes an enemy of God. (James 4:4)

And now, Israel, what does the Lord your God ask of you but to fear the Lord your God, to walk in obedience to Him, to love Him, to serve the Lord your God with all your heart and with all your soul, and to observe the Lord's commands and decrees that I am giving you today for your own good? (Deuteronomy 10:12-13)

In fact, this is love for God: to keep His commands. And His commands are not burdensome, for everyone born of God overcomes the world. This is the victory that has overcome the world, even our faith. Who is it that overcomes the world? Only the one who believes that Jesus is the Son of God. (1 John 5:3-5)

Whoever has my commands and keeps them is the one who loves me. The one who loves me will be loved by my Father, and I too will love them and show my-self to them. (John 14:21)

Therefore, I urge you, brothers and sisters, in view of God's mercy, to offer your bodies as a living sacrifice, holy and pleasing to God—this is your true and proper worship. (Romans 12:1)

Whoever does not love does not know God, because God is love. (1 John 4:8)

I love those who love me, and those who seek me find me. With me are riches and honor, enduring wealth and pros-perity. (Proverbs 8:17-18)

Those who know your name trust in you, for you, Lord, have never forsaken those who seek you. (Psalm 9:10)

If my people, who are called by my name, will humble themselves and pray and seek my face and turn from their wicked ways, then I will hear from heaven, and I will forgive their sin and will heal their land. (2 Chronicles 7:14)

Submit yourselves, then, to God. Resist the devil, and he will flee from you. Come near to God and He will come near to you. Wash your hands, you sinners, and purify your hearts, you double-minded. (James 4:7-8)

[Jesus said,] "No one can serve two masters. Either you will hate the one and love the other, or you will be devoted to the one and despise the other. You cannot serve both God and money." (Matthew 6:24)

Seek the Lord while He may be found; call on Him while He is near. Let the wicked forsake their ways and the unrighteous their thoughts. Let them turn to the Lord, and He will have mercy on them, and to our God, for He will freely pardon. (Isaiah 55:6-7)

Trust in the Lord and do good; dwell in the land and enjoy safe pasture. Take delight in the Lord, and He will give you the desires of your heart. Commit your way to the Lord; trust in Him and He will do this: He will make your righteous reward shine like the dawn, your vindication like the noonday sun. (Psalm 37:3-6)

And I will put my Spirit in you and move you to follow my decrees and be careful to keep my laws. (Ezekiel 36:27)

Trust in the Lord with all your heart and lean not on your own understanding; in all your ways submit to Him, and He will make your paths straight. Do not be wise in your own eyes; fear the Lord and shun evil. This will bring health to your body and nourishment to your bones. (Proverbs 3:5-8)

My flesh and my heart may fail, but God is the strength of my heart and my portion forever. (Psalm 73:26)

But whoever loves God is known by
God. (1 Corinthians 8:3)

Then I saw another angel flying in
midair, and he had the eternal gospel
to proclaim to those who live on the
earth—to every nation, tribe, language
and people. He said in a loud voice,
"Fear God and give Him glory, because
the hour of His judgement has come.
Worship Him who made the heavens,
the earth, the sea and the springs of
water." (Revelation 14:6-7)

[Jesus said,] "And do not call anyone on
earth 'father,' for you have one Father,
and He is in heaven." (Matthew 23:9)

Just love Him with all of your heart even though
you can't see Him. He loves you more than you
know and is merciful, gracious, and forgiving. He
and Jesus are one. The loving qualities of Jesus stem
from the Father. We may not be able to see God,
and we weren't here when Jesus walked the earth
as a man and a servant, but the bible says, "blessed
are those who have not seen and yet have believed"

(John 20:29). We have the Word of God which is another name for Jesus (Revelation 19:13), so we can paint a picture of our loving Savior. We may not have been able to see Jesus, but we can read about His heart. There is no other teacher in the history of mankind that can even come close to the heart of Jesus. The Father said, "This is my Son, whom I love; with Him I am well pleased" (Matthew 3:17).

God will know that we earnestly love Him with all of our hearts if we obey Him and put Him first in our lives. If you are a father, I'm sure that you know that your child loves you when he or she respects you and isn't rebellious. Those of us who have earthly fathers are aware that our fathers know that we love them when we listen to them and follow their guidance. They know that we love them when we communicate with them on a regular basis. God the Father wants us to talk to Him regularly about anything and everything that is going on in our lives through prayer. Please don't brush God aside. Include Him in every aspect of your life. Make time during the day to pray to Him, He deserves it. Lastly, the Father will know that we love Him deeply if we love Jesus because Jesus said He and the Father are one.

CHAPTER FOURTEEN

Loving Our Neighbors

"Love the Lord your God with all your heart and with all your soul and with all your mind and with all your strength." The second is this: "Love your neighbor as yourself." There is no commandment greater than these. (Mark 12:30-31)

Finally, all of you, be like-minded, be sympathetic, love one another, be compassionate and humble. (1 Peter 3:8)

Therefore encourage one another and build each other up, just as in fact you are doing. (1 Thessalonians 5:11)

No one should seek their own good, but the good of others. (1 Corinthians 10:24)

Carry each other's burdens, and in this way you will fulfill the law of Christ. (Galatians 6:2)

For the entire law is fulfilled in keeping this one command: "Love your neighbor as yourself." (Galatians 5:14)

So in everything, do to others what you would have them do to you, for this sums up the Law and the Prophets. (Matthew 7:12)

Keep on loving one another as brothers and sisters. Do not forget to show hospitality to strangers, for by so doing some people have shown hospitality to angels without knowing it. (Hebrews 13:1-2)

Do nothing out of selfish ambition or vain conceit. Rather, in humility value others above yourselves, not looking to your own interests but each of you to the interests of the others. (Philippians 2:3-4)

Each of us should please our neighbors for their good, to build them up. (Romans 15:2)

Therefore let us stop passing judgement on one another. Instead, make up your mind not to put any stumbling block or obstacle in the way of a brother or sister. (Romans 14:13)

Therefore, as we have opportunity, let us do good to all people, especially to those who belong to the family of believers. (Galatians 6:10)

Bear with each other and forgive one another if any of you has a grievance against someone. Forgive as the Lord forgave you. (Colossians 3:13)

Above all, love each other deeply, because love covers over a multitude of sins. (1 Peter 4:8)

Love does no harm to a neighbor. Therefore love is the fulfillment of the law. (Romans 13:10)

[Jesus said,] "A new command I give you: Love one another. As I have loved you, so you must love one another. By this everyone will know that you are my disciples, if you love one another." (John 13:34-35)

Be devoted to one another in love. Honor one another above yourselves. (Romans 12:10)

Anyone who withholds kindness from a friend forsakes the fear of the Almighty. (Job 6:14)

May the Lord make your love increase and overflow for each other and for everyone else, just as ours does for you. (1 Thessalonians 3:12)

The commandments, "You shall not commit adultery," "You shall not murder," "You shall not steal," "You shall not covet," and whatever other command there may be, are summed up in this one command: "Love your neighbor as yourself." (Romans 13:9)

For this is the message you heard from the beginning: We should love one another. (1 John 3:11)

Dear friends, let us love one another, for love comes from God. Everyone who loves has been born of God and knows God. (1 John 4:7)

Accept one another, then, just as Christ accepted you, in order to bring praise to God. (Romans 15:7)

For this very reason, make every effort to add to your faith goodness; and to goodness, knowledge; and to knowledge, self-control; and to self-control, perseverance; and to perseverance, godliness; and to godliness, mutual affection; and to mutual affection, love. (2 Peter 1:5-7)

Be merciful, just as your Father is merciful. (Luke 6:36)

If anyone has material possessions and sees a brother or sister in need but has not pity on them, how can the love of God be in that person? (1 John 3:17)

Now that I, your Lord and Teacher, have washed your feet, you also should wash one another's feet. (John 13:14)

This is how we know what love is: Jesus Christ laid down His life for us. And we ought to lay down our lives for our brothers and sisters. (1 John 3:16)

Then Peter came to Jesus and asked, "Lord, how many times shall I forgive my brother or sister who sins against me? Up to seven times?" Jesus answered, "I tell you, not seven times, seventy-seven times." (Matthew 18:21-22)

[Jesus said,] "My command is this: Love each other as I have loved you. Greater love has no one than this: to lay down one's life for one's friends." (John 15:12-13)

Be careful not to neglect your friends and your neighbors, because we know all too well that it is easy for a friend to become an enemy. We are to put others before ourselves. Jesus basically said if you desire to be first, you might as well be a slave. We are called to serve one another. Many times, we are going to be tested. Are we going to choose selfishness or generosity? Are we going to choose love or fear? That is one truth I learned from one of my pastors, Daryl Kyle Sr.; the opposite of love is fear, not hate. We are born into selfishness. We learn at a very young age the word, "mine." We are born into sin, but there is hope through God. We can change and be a new creation. We can bury the old self and be renewed in Christ.

CHAPTER FIFTEEN

Loving Our Enemies

~Words of Jesus~

You have heard that it was said, "Love your neighbor and hate your enemy." But I tell you, love your enemies and pray for those who persecute you, that you may be children of your Father in heaven. He causes His sun to rise on the evil and the good, and sends rain on the righteous and the unrighteous.

If you love those who love you, what reward will you get: Are not even the tax collectors doing that? And if you greet only your own people, what are you doing more than others? Do not even pagans do that? Be perfect, therefore, as your heavenly Father is perfect. (Matthew 5:43-48)

But to you who are listening I say: Love your enemies, do good to those who hate you, bless those who curse you, pray for those who mistreat you. If someone slaps you on one cheek, turn to them the other also. If someone takes your coat, do not withhold your shirt from them. Give to everyone who asks you, and if anyone takes what belongs to you, do not demand it back. Do to others as you would have them do to you.

If you love those who love you, what credit is that to you? Even sinners love those who love them. And if you lend to those from whom you expect repayment, what credit is that to you? Even sinners lend to sinners, expecting to be repaid in full. But love your enemies, do good to them, and lend to them without expecting to get anything back. Then your reward will be great, and you will be children of the Most High, because He is kind to the ungrateful and wicked. Be merciful, just as your Father is merciful.

Do not judge, and you will not be judged. Do not condemn, and you will not be condemned. Forgive, and you will be forgiven. Give, and it will be given to you. A good measure, pressed down, shaken together and running over, will be poured into your lap. For with the measure you use, it will be measured to you. (Luke 6:27-38)

So in everything, do to others what you would have them do to you, for this sums up the Law and the Prophets. (Matthew 7:12)

Father, forgive them for they do not know what they are doing. (Luke 23:34)

~Other Verses on Loving Our Enemies~

Bless those who persecute you; bless and do not curse. (Romans 12:14)

If your enemy is hungry, give him food to eat; if he is thirsty, give him water to drink. In doing this, you will heap burning coals on his head, and the Lord will reward you. (Proverbs 25:21-22)

[When Stephen was being stoned to death] he fell on his knees and cried out, "Lord, do not hold this sin against them." When he had said this, he fell asleep. (Acts 7:60)

Do not gloat when your enemy falls; when they stumble, do not let your heart rejoice, or the Lord will see and disapprove and turn His wrath away from them. (Proverbs 24:17-18)

A gentle answer turns away wrath, but
a harsh word stirs up anger. (Proverbs
15:1)

Forget the former things; do not dwell
on the past. (Isaiah 43:18)

Now this is one of our greatest challenges as believers in Christ, to love our enemies. It definitely goes against human nature. When we think of the wickedness that is present in today's world, it's almost impossible to love some of these people. I am fully aware of the terrorism that exists today, and I pray for those who are being persecuted, tortured, and killed. But I also pray for the terrorists, that they might be converted. Remember how Saul persecuted and killed believers in Christ and was then converted and became a great apostle for the Lord.

For me, I have decided to focus on enemies that may be in my surroundings day by day near my hometown. I try to stay vigilant, even when I get out of the house just to go to the store. Personally, I can't think of any serious enemies I have that could possibly be a threat to me, but when I go out into the world, I never know what could possibly happen.

I have prayed for my family, friends, enemies and strangers on many occasions. I really don't have any conflict with anyone today, and I thank God for that. I believe it is a blessing. Proverbs 16:7 states, "when the Lord takes pleasure in anyone's way, He causes their enemies to make peace with them." This is part of the peace and rest I spoke of earlier that I have been experiencing.

I believe that if we truly seek and pray that God's will be done in our lives, it will happen. If we pray for the strength and ability to love our enemies, it will be fulfilled. There are people in my life that I considered family even though they weren't blood relatives that cut ties with me due to my past behaviors. I believe I will see them again and have a relationship with them in the future, because the Lord is the loving God of restoration.

I also believe that if we seek first the kingdom of God, and pray earnestly for God to be forever present in us, that too will be fulfilled. "Every good and perfect gift is from above" (James 1:17). When I was younger I knew the verse, "if the Son sets you free, you will be free indeed" (John 8:36). But I was ignorant of the freedom God is speaking of in the verse. I basically thought I could just do whatever I wanted. I now believe the freedom He is speaking of is freedom from fear, freedom from the devil, his angels, and demons, by putting on the armor of God; freedom from an unsound mind, freedom from idols that alienate us from God, freedom from being attached to this world, freedom from guilt and shame, freedom from condemnation, freedom from anger and strife, freedom from false teachers, freedom from confusion, and freedom from feeling alone.

In the practice of loving our enemies or loving people that just have a way of irritating us; God will speak to us (His children) in those moments if we listen closely. It has happened to me. That still small voice that says, "Forgive them for they do not know what they are doing." "Do not judge them or you will be judged." "How can you love me who you cannot see if you don't love your brother or sister who you can see?"

Be patient and remember, "He who began a good work in you will carry it on to completion until the day of Christ Jesus" (Philippians 1:6). The work in me hasn't been completed. I look at each day now as a test. I may know His word but the question is, will I practice it? Someone tomorrow may ask me if they can borrow a substantial amount of money. If I have the amount asked, will I loan it or not? The

Lord will not give us more than we can handle. I know that when I have gone through some really difficult times, the hardest times in fact, I was at my wit's end. I cursed God in those moments. I didn't understand during that time that I was being disciplined. All I knew is that I was going through very serious emotional pain. But I finally learned. I finally realized I had to make some serious changes in my life. I finally realized I had to ask for help from God to make those changes.

So I encourage you to consider the next three verses:

> Examine yourselves to see whether you are in the faith; test yourselves. Do you not realize that Christ Jesus is in you—unless, of course, you fail the test? (2 Corinthians 13:5)

> And without faith it is impossible to please God, because anyone who comes to Him must believe that He exists and that He rewards those who earnestly seek Him. (Hebrews 11:6)

> In the same way, faith by itself, if it is
> not accompanied by action, is dead.
> (James 2:17)

Don't get me wrong. It's not like I've mastered everything I have written about. This book may not only challenge the reader, but is challenging to me as I write it. Jesus has plainly said, "If you love Me you will keep My commands" (John 14:15). Yes, He gave us two: Love God the Father and love our neighbors as ourselves. But in addition He also said in John 14:23, "Anyone who loves Me will obey My teaching. My Father will love them, and We will come to them and make Our home with them."

Jesus taught us many things and told us how we should live. I think it would be in our best interest to do as He says. I, personally, do not want to stand before God and be reminded of Matthew 7:23, "I never knew you, away from me you evildoer!"

> Therefore, since we are receiving a
> kingdom that cannot be shaken, let us
> be thankful, and so worship God ac-
> ceptably with reverence and awe, for
> our "God is a consuming fire." (Hebrews
> 12:28-29)

CHAPTER SIXTEEN

Loving Ourselves

I praise you because I am fearfully and wonderfully made; your works are wonderful, I know that full well. (Psalm 139:14)

The one who gets wisdom loves life; the one who cherishes understanding will soon prosper. (Proverbs 19:8)

After all, no one ever hated their own body, but they feed and care for their body, just as Christ does the church. (Ephesians 5:29)

[Jesus said,] "Very truly I tell you, whoever believes in Me will do the works I have been doing, and they will do even greater things than these, because I am going to the Father." (John 14:12)

If God loves us so much, unconditionally, we should love ourselves; not in a conceited or self-worship way, but we should care about ourselves as Christ cares for the church. If God is gracious and merciful to us, and forgives us, we should be gracious, merciful and forgiving to ourselves as well. Psalm 103:11-12 states, "For as high as the heavens are above the earth, so great is His love for those who fear Him; as far as the east is from the west, so far has He removed our transgressions from us." If God has remembered our sins no more and has removed our transgressions from us, why should we then dwell on past mistakes?

I believe many believers struggle with guilt, shame, and self-condemnation because the devil wants to keep them from the Spirit of truth that tells us we are free and have been forgiven. The devil will always try to discourage us and steal our joy. The joy of the Lord is our strength. Our own joy isn't our strength. It is a false joy. We need joy that comes from above. True joy comes from standing on the truth of the word of God. We have to make a choice to be strong in the Lord and in His mighty power. Daily, we have to put on the armor of God, as mentioned in chapter 6 of Ephesians, that will protect us from the devil, his angels, and demons:

> Put on the full armor of God, so that you can take your stand against the devil's schemes. For our struggle is not against flesh and blood, but against the rulers, against the authorities, against the powers of this dark world and against the spiritual forces of evil in the heavenly realms. Therefore put on the full armor of God, so that when the day of evil comes, you may be able to stand your ground, and after you have done everything, to stand. Stand firm then, with the belt of truth buckled around your waist, with the breastplate of righteousness in place, and with your feet fitted with the readiness that comes from the gospel of peace. In addition to all this, take the helmet of salvation

and the sword of the Spirit, which is the
word of God. (Ephesians 6:11-17)

Loving ourselves means having healthy boundaries with others. We don't just become a "loving doormat" to others. Sometimes, a person may need reproof or rebuke. "Whoever turns a sinner from the error of their way will save them from death and cover over a multitude of sins" (James 5:20). Those who wish to control or manipulate others do not act in love. One of the fruits of the Spirit is self-control and we have to put ourselves in check so not to try to control or manipulate others ourselves. If we don't put ourselves in check, I'm sure the good Lord will. We are to hate what is evil and cling to what is good (Romans 12:9). We are not to hate the person but the evil.

We have to learn how to communicate effectively in heated confrontations. The power of God, Jesus and the Holy Spirit will help us with this. God can give us peace and patience in turmoil. He can give us a calm spirit. We are to avoid anger, strife, dissensions, and contentions. There will definitely be times when we will get angry. Remember, the bible doesn't say , love is not angered. It says , love is not *easily* angered. The bible says God is slow to anger (Psalm 86:15), but we have to be very careful when it comes to anger. It can be very destructive. I suggest following what the next verse says:

> But now you must also rid yourselves of all such things as these: anger, rage, malice, slander, and filthy language from your lips. (Colossians 3:8)

I'm well aware of the story of Jesus when He went on a rampage and entered the temple courts and drove out all who were buying and selling there. He overturned the tables of the money changers and the benches of those selling doves and said, "It is written, My house will be called a house of prayer, but you are making it a den of robbers." (Matthew 21:12-13) He was angry alright, but I don't believe we are to follow this type of behavior in our modern day. He was God in the flesh and was cleansing the temple.

I believe another way of taking care of ourselves is by obeying rules and laws. We have responsibilities towards the higher powers:

> Let everyone be subject to the governing authorities, for there is no authority except that which God has established.

The authorities that exist have been established by God. Consequently, whoever rebels against the authority is rebelling against what God has instituted, and those who do so will bring judgement on themselves. For rulers hold no terror for those who do right, but for those who do wrong. Do you want to be free from fear of the one in authority? Then do what is right and you will be commended. For the one in authority is God's servant for your good. But if you do wrong, be afraid, for rulers do not bear the sword for no reason. They are God's servants, agents of wrath to bring punishment on the wrongdoer. Therefore it is necessary to submit to the authorities, not only because of possible punishment but also as a matter of conscience. (Romans 13:1-5)

There is a reward right here on earth when we follow rules and laws. It puts us in good standing with those in authority over us and even those around us. If your neighbor knows of you to be a peaceful person who doesn't start trouble or get into trouble, you may be more respected and accepted. If you do good, good will come back to you. We reap what we sow. We are the light of the world, and if anyone recognizes good works in us and commends us, our Father in heaven is glorified.

By loving God and being reverent towards Him, we love ourselves. By loving our neighbors as ourselves, we love ourselves; and definitely by loving our enemies we love ourselves. A good way to love our enemies is by looking at our own shortcomings and what we have been guilty of. Jesus said, "Let any one of you who is without sin be the first to throw a stone at her (the adulteress)." By reading the Word of God and following what Jesus has told us to do, we love ourselves. By prayer, meditation, and fasting, we love ourselves. We love ourselves by looking in the mirror and telling ourselves, I am a child of God and a joint-heir with Christ; loved, forgiven, free, and called to do great things in His name.

CHAPTER SEVENTEEN

The Second Coming and Heaven

~The Second Coming~

But the day of the Lord will come like a thief. The heavens will disappear with a roar; the elements will be destroyed by fire, and the earth and everything done in it will be laid bare.

> Since everything will be destroyed in this way, what kind of people ought you to be? You ought to live holy and

godly lives as you look forward to the day of God and speed its coming. That day will bring about the destruction of the heavens by fire, and the elements will melt in the heat. But in keeping with His promise we are looking forward to a new heaven and a new earth, where righteousness dwells. (2 Peter 3:10-13)

For as lightning that comes from the east is visible even in the west, so will be the coming of the Son of Man. Wherever there is a carcass, there the vultures will gather.

Immediately after the distress of those days, the sun will be darkened and the moon will not give its light; the stars will fall from the sky, and the heavenly bodies will be shaken.

Then will appear the sign of the Son of Man in heaven. And then all the peoples of the earth will mourn when they see the Son of Man coming on the clouds of heaven, with power and great glory. And He will send His angels with a loud trumpet call, and they will gather His elect from the four winds, from one end of the heavens to the other. (Matthew 24:27-31)

For the Lord Himself will come down from heaven, with a loud command, with the voice of the archangel and with the trumpet call of God, and the dead in Christ will rise first. After that, we who are still alive and are left will be caught up together with them in the clouds to meet the Lord in the air. And so we will be with the Lord forever. (1 Thessalonians 4:16-17)

I saw Heaven standing open and there before me was a white horse, whose rider is called Faithful and True. With justice he judges and wages war. His eyes are like blazing fire, and on His head are many crowns. He has a name written on Him that no one knows but He Himself. He is dressed in a robe dipped in blood and His name is the Word of God. The armies of heaven were following Him, riding on white horses and dressed in fine linen, white and clean. Coming out of His mouth is a sharp sword with which to strike down the nations. "He will rule them with an iron scepter." He treads the winepress of the fury of the wrath of God Almighty. (Revelation 19:11-15)

~Heaven~

By the word of the Lord the heavens were made, their starry host by the breath of His mouth. (Psalm 33:6)

Once, on being asked by the Pharisees when the kingdom of God would come, Jesus replied, "The coming of the kingdom of God is not something that can be observed, nor will people say, 'Here it is,' or 'There it is,' because the kingdom of God is in your midst." (Luke 17:20-21)

And Jesus said, "Truly I tell you, unless you change and become like little children, you will never enter the kingdom of heaven." (Matthew 18:3)

[Jesus said,] "For I tell you that unless your righteousness surpasses that of the Pharisees and the teachers of the law, you will certainly not enter the kingdom of heaven." (Matthew 5:20)

Then Jesus said to His disciples, "Truly I tell you, it is hard for someone who is rich to enter the kingdom of heaven." (Matthew 19:23)

Jesus said, "Not everyone who says to me, 'Lord, Lord,' will enter the kingdom of heaven, but only the one who does the will of my Father who is in heaven." (Matthew 7:21)

[Jesus said,] "Truly I tell you, anyone who will not receive the kingdom of God like a little child will never enter it." (Mark 10:15)

Jesus replied, "Very truly I tell you, no one can see the kingdom of God unless they are born again." (John 3:3)

Jesus answered, "Very truly I tell you, no one can enter the kingdom of God unless they are born of water and the Spirit." (John 3:5)

This is how it will be at the end of the age. The angels will come and separate the wicked from the righteous and throw them into the blazing furnace, where there will be weeping and gnashing of teeth. (Matthew 13:49-50)

[Jesus] said, "The knowledge of the secrets of the kingdom of God has been given to you, but to others I speak in parables, so that, though seeing, they may not see; though hearing, they may not understand." (Luke 8:10)

Jesus said, "Let the little children come to me, and do not hinder them, for the kingdom of heaven belongs to such as these." (Matthew 19:14)

"Truly I tell you," Jesus said to them, "no one who has left home or wife or brothers or sisters or parents or children for the sake of the kingdom of God will fail to receive many times as much in this age, and in the age to come eternal life." (Luke 18:29-30)

Jesus said, "My Father's house has many rooms; if that were not so, would I have told you that I am going there to prepare a place for you? And if I go and prepare a place for you, I will come back and take you to be with Me that you also may be where I am." (John 14:2-3)

However, as it is written: "What no eye has seen, what no ear has heard, and what no human mind has conceived"— the things God has prepared for those who love Him—these are the things God has revealed to us by His Spirit.

The Spirit searches all things of God. (1 Corinthians 2:9-10)

Jesus said to her, "I am the resurrection and the life. The one who believes in Me will live, even though they die; and whoever lives by believing in Me will never die. Do you believe this?" (John 11:25-26)

Now I have to stop for a second here. I want you to realize what Jesus said. Whoever lives by believing in Him shall never die! Do you believe this? I do! I believe I shall never die, because Jesus Christ said so. I stand on the word of God only now, not what others say to me. Jesus Christ tells us, "For you have one Instructor, the Messiah" (Matthew 23:10). Most people would think this isn't a realistic belief but Jesus is trying to tell us that those who believe in Him will live, even though they die. Why do you think he asked the question, "Do you believe this?" He knew many would doubt this spiritual truth. Whoever lives by believing in Jesus Christ shall never die. People are either going to believe everything Jesus said or they are not.

When Christ, who is your life, appears, then you also will appear with Him in glory. (Colossians 3:4)

> For we know that if the earthly tent we live in is destroyed, we have a building from God, an eternal house in heaven, not built by human hands. (2 Corinthians 5:1)

> Whoever has ears, let them hear what the Spirit says to the churches. To the one who is victorious, I will give some of the hidden manna. I will also give that person a white stone with a new name written on it, known only to the one who receives it. (Revelation 2:17)

~Throne of God in Heaven~

Revelation 4

> After this I looked, and there before me was a door standing open in heaven. And the voice I had first heard speaking to me like a trumpet said, "Come

up here, and I will show you what must take place after this." At once I was in the Spirit, and there before me was a throne in heaven with someone sitting on it. And the one who sat there had the appearance of jasper and ruby. A rainbow that shone like an emerald encircled the throne. Surrounding the throne were twenty-four other thrones, and seated on them were twenty-four elders. They were dressed in white and had crowns of gold on their heads. From the throne came flashes of lightning, rumblings and peals of thunder. In front of the throne, seven lamps were blazing. These are the seven spirits of God. Also in front of the throne there was what looked like a sea of glass, clear as crystal.

In the center, around the throne, were four living creatures, and they were covered with eyes, in front and back. The first living creature was like a lion, the second was like an ox, the third had a face like a man, the fourth was like a flying eagle. Each of the four living creatures had six wings and was covered with eyes all around, even under its wings. Day and night they never stop saying:

"Holy, holy, holy is the Lord God Almighty, who was, and is, and is to come."

Whenever the living creatures give glory, honor and thanks to Him who sits on the throne and who lives for ever and ever, the twenty-four elders fall down before Him who sits on the throne and worship Him who lives for ever and ever. They lay their crowns before the throne and say:

"You are worthy, our Lord and God, to receive glory and honor and power, for you created all things, and by your will they were created and have their being." (Revelation 4)

And I saw the dead, great and small, standing before the throne, and books were opened. Another book was opened, which is the book of life. The dead were judged according to what they had done as recorded in the books. The sea gave up the dead that were in it, and death and Hades gave up the dead that were in them, and each person was judged according to what they had done. Then death and Hades were thrown into the lake of fire. The lake of fire is the second death. Anyone whose name was not found written in the book of life was thrown into the lake of fire. (Revelation 20:12-15)

Then I saw "a new heaven and a new earth," for the first heaven and the first earth had passed away, and there was no longer any sea. I saw the Holy City, the new Jerusalem, coming down out of heaven from God, prepared as a bride beautifully dressed for her husband. (Revelation 21:1-2)

He will wipe away every tear from their eyes. There will be no more death or mourning or crying or pain, for the old order of things has passed away. (Revelation 21:4)

Then the angel showed me the river of the water of life, as clear as crystal, flowing from the throne of God and of the Lamb down the middle of the great street of the city. On each side of the river stood the tree of life, bearing twelve crops of fruit, yielding its fruit every month. And the leaves of the tree are for the healing of the nations. (Revelation 22:1-2)

He who testifies to these things says, "Yes, I am coming soon." Amen. Come, Lord Jesus. (Revelation 22:20)

What a glorious day that will be, when Jesus returns! "The Lord is not slow concerning His promise, as some understand slowness. Instead, He is patient with us, not wanting anyone to perish, but everyone to come to repentance" (2 Peter 3:9). Some bible versions say that in the Father's house are many rooms, some say in the Father's house are many mansions. Whether in a small room or in a mansion, I will be happy just to be with my Father and Jesus in heaven. A place of pure bliss where there is no more pain or mourning or conflict; a place of perfect peace. We have some idea of what heaven is going to be like, but I think God has so much more prepared for us that we cannot even fathom. I believe it will be the greatest surprise ever, and it will be an eternal surprise! What am I saying? Who am I kidding? Heaven is unfathomable!

So, is the Lord in you? Have you been blessed with the Holy Spirit who can teach you all things and help you love others as Jesus commanded? Do you love God with all your heart, soul, strength, and mind? Do you love your neighbors? Are you making an effort to love your enemies? Do you love your neighbor as yourself? Do you love God as yourself? He is our Father and wants an intimate relationship with us. Any father would want to be loved by his son or daughter. God wants us to love Him just the same. Jesus said, "do not call anyone on earth 'father,' for you have one Father, and He is in heaven" (Matthew 23:9)" Our God is a jealous God (Exodus 34:14). He wants to be number one in our hearts, minds, and lives.

All scripture aside, when I think of "living in love," to me it means to have love be a constant focus at all times. I truly believe we are never going to attain a high level of loving others, especially enemies, without the help of God the Father, Jesus Christ, the Holy Spirit, and prayer. We need to be praying God's will be done as it is in heaven. We need to pray with others and also in secret.

I hope you have been encouraged and edified by reading this book. I hope it blesses you and is a tool to light a fire in your heart. I know I have learned a lot just by writing it. Remember, He who began a good work in us is faithful to complete it. God will always be there for us even if we cannot see Him yet. Never forget that. We can call on Him day or night and talk to Him about anything. That is what prayer actually is, just talking to our Father.

I pray the Lord bless you, protect you, teach you, help you, provide for you, comfort you and heal you of any wounds or scars you may have in your heart. But most of all, I pray the Father's will be done in your life. His plan for our lives is so much better than our plans. Give Him some credit, He created everything! Put on the armor of God but remember you are wearing shoes of the gospel of peace. May His angels surround you at all times. Practice hope, faith, and love. But practice loving the most, for it is the greatest of the three (1 Corinthians 13:13). Think of heaven often and live in love so that you can live in God, and He can live in you. In conclusion, I just want to encourage you to pray for the power to love your enemies, because <u>if you can love an enemy, you can love anyone</u>. To God, Jesus Christ, and the Holy Spirit be all the glory and honor eternally. Amen.

Notes

Scripture reference search sources:

www.biblestudytools.com
www.dailyverses.net
www.bible.knowing-jesus.com
www.biblereasons.com
www.openbible.info
www.christianquotes.info
www.everydayservant.com

Chapter 16: Loving Ourselves
"Boundaries" – www.gotquestions.com
Word definitions taken from:
King James Version Dictionary

About the Author

Chad Tucker has been a believer in Jesus Christ since he was fifteen years old. He began studying the bible when he was seventeen years old and started attending Maranatha Chapel in San Diego, California. Like a prodigal son, he left the faith shortly after his divorce at the age of twenty-three but soon came back to the Lord at the age of twenty-five. Although he attended church, he had not completely surrendered his life to the Lord. He suffered for many years dealing with a mental illness and drug addiction but is now sober, stable, and the Lord is transforming and renewing his mind.

He became a born again believer on January 23, 2017 and rededicated his life to Christ shortly after. He now attends a small church called Calvary Chapel Perfect Love in Spring Valley, California and is involved with another local ministry called

The Training Center which ministers to people coming out of jail and prison. He presently works as an assistant manager of a faith-based sober living apartment complex run by The Training Center in Spring Valley.